NO SS

NEW TY

NO ACCESS

NEW YORK CITY

THE CITY'S HIDDEN TREASURES, HAUNTS, AND FORGOTTEN PLACES

JAMIE MCDONALD

Globe
Pequot

GUILFORD, CONNECTICUT

Globe
Pequot

An imprint of The Rowman & Littlefield Publishing Group, Inc.
4501 Forbes Blvd., Ste. 200
Lanham, MD 20706
www.rowman.com

Distributed by NATIONAL BOOK NETWORK

British Library Cataloguing in Publication Information available
Library of Congress Cataloging-in-Publication Data available

ISBN 978-1-4930-2807-8 (paperback)
ISBN 978-1-4930-2808-5 (e-book)

♾™ The paper used in this publication meets the minimum requirements of American National Standard for Information Sciences—Permanence of Paper for Printed Library Materials, ANSI/NISO Z39.48-1992

Printed in the United States of America

For the Hammonds family

CONTENTS

INTRODUCTION

Everyone likes to be in the know about their own neck of the woods. New Yorker's are especially guilty of this human trait. They love swapping stories with each other, at times almost trying to one up another on their know-how of a neighborhood or local institution. Be it little known factoids, behind the curtain tales, or some quirky under the radar place only known to locals, everyone enjoys an insider's look to what makes their part of the world so unique.

No Access New York City is a collection these kind of anecdotes surely to make everyone look at New York City in a new light. Subjects include places off-limits, rarely visited or purposely hidden from outsiders. But this is not just an "Insider's-insider's guide," rather, there are plenty of places universally intriguing to locals, first time visitors and those who have never even stepped foot in the New York City.

Unfortunately some of the most fascinating places in New York City are off-limits to the general public. We however got behind the gates to show you firsthand some of these places.

Locals will discover fresh finds right under their noses while out-of-towners, can get a chance to experience "real New York"—not tourist traps. Few travel books profile places like this because they tend to gloss over out-of-the-way spots for "safe bets" and more conventional locales.

And in a city with hundreds of museums and cultural institutions, many of them can fall off the radar and get nary a notice, so we have included some the best hidden gems which are unique, under-appreciated and have an added bonus: free of crowds.

So there is a little of everything here—the forbidden, exclusive and unknown—all for you to discover on your couch, in person, or in some cases right in your own neck of the woods.

77 WATER STREET

Across the Manhattan skyline, behemoth skyscrapers of glass and steel are a necessity in a city so compact. But sometimes they tend to visually blur into one another. And in a city where time is money and space is a highly-valued commodity, there often seems little room for fun and whimsy; that is until one gazes upon 77 Water Street.

It starts out on the roof, for there, rather astonishingly, is what looks to be a World War I era airplane complete with its own runway and lights. Countless people have inquired why it is there, in a way answering their own question because it is merely there for one reason: to invoke a little diversion in a sometimes tedious city roofscape.

This and other visual treats at 77 Water Street are part of a credo for its owners/developers, The William Kaufman Organization. This third generation, family-owned real estate development company has been doting the New York City Skyline for decades and putting little creative adornments or "twists" on their buildings which has become a bit of a credo for them.

It started with founder William Kaufman Sr. who felt people spent so much time in their workplace more should be done to humanize it. So along with his sons, Robert and Melvyn, they started to incorporate bits of visual whimsy into their buildings to stimulate the mind and soul. 77 Water is perhaps their crowning achievement.

The bi-plane on the roof is only the beginning. Just take a look under the lobby's atrium along the building's ultra-modern gleaming glass lobby entrance. Almost incredulously is what appears to be an old-fashioned general store complete with a red and yellow awning and vintage advertisements. It is fully open for business selling candy coffee, lotto tickets and just about anything else in a "modern" store. One might think this little shop is an old-world holdout refusing to budge for the 26 floor tower, but it was actually built as part of the development, again giving what could have been be a bit of an antiseptic area, more of a human touch.

Along with the general store, 77 Water Street's street level is peppered with numerous art installations that seem to push the boundaries of staid art. They include the "Month of June," by George Adamy large translucent lollipops looking circles that double as swivel benches. Nearby, look carefully at the rock bed towards the sidewalk and you'll see metal herring like fish swimming upstream in a large bed of pebbles. It's part of an installation entitled, "Herring-Like Fishes Swimming Upstream" by Pamela Waters.

Even part of the building itself is its own art installation. Entitled "Rejected Skin," the

Photos courtesy of The William Kaufman Organization

art piece consists of giant crushed aluminum panels discarded from the building's construction.

As for the rooftop plane, it is a 1916 World War I British Sopwith Camel replica designed by Rudolph de Harak and constructed by sculptor William Tarr. In 1969 it had to be lifted by crane to its location. This art installation however was done not for the benefit of those who work at 77 Water Street. The Kaufmann's say it was solely done for the entertainment of the building's neighbors. Imagine the puzzled stares and maddening questions the sight must have generated before the age of the internet search.

As for the plane, after over 40 years on top of the building it is not going anywhere. Part of the idea of the piece was to let us slowly deteriorate due to the elements—until it is no more.

767 THIRD AVENUE

People living and working in midtown Manhattan can see the Kaufaman's unique touch at 767 Third Avenue at 48th Street. First off, there is the enormous three story chessboard above the public courtyard, where each chess piece is about two and a half feet. And yes, it indeed works. Pieces are moved weekly with a cherrypicker. A nearby flag lets passerbys know which side gets the next move. So who's playing? Actually no one. The moves are a kind of replay of well-known chess matches in history.

The 42-story office building also stands out from its counterparts due to the heavy use of brick and oak wood on its main entrance, rather than the usual glass and steel accruements.

Then there is the 1929 Ford Pickup truck sitting and stagecoach in outdoor lobby area, again going with the Kaufmann's credo, "Why Not?" That also goes for the steel foot prints walking along on the otherwise boring sidewalk ventilation grating.

AMATEUR COMEDY CLUB

Far from the lights on Broadway, in the much more tranquil Murray Hill neighborhood, stands a couple of well-maintained carriage houses on 36th Street. Few walking by have an inkling of what goes on inside—even less would surmise it is a theatre.

Behind these humble double barn doors is the Amateur Comedy Club; not only the oldest continuously performing theatrical company in the United States but also one of the oldest private clubs in New York City.

But one will not find its performances advertised or tickets sold. The club is solely open for members of the club and their friends to enjoy theatre and camaraderie. As their mission statement eloquently explains, "Members come from every discipline and industry, from finance to musicians to professional actors, who wish to hone their skills and showcase their talent. The one common thread is that we are all passionate about theater."

And are they passionate. Most of the sets, productions, and acting are done by members of the club and members of the all-women's theatrical group The Snarks. The club is often abuzz with rehearsals, set building and home-cooked dinners. As club president Steve Goldberg puts it, "The shows are a vessel for us to have community." One can feel it at their social events. Unlike many social clubs, people are not here to hustle for business, clients or social network. They come from all walks of life and age groups. Member William Brown says "It's funny, there are some friends here, and I don't even know what they do for a living."

Membership into the club is for men only and they must be recommended by another member. At any given time, there are only 100 members and around 250 associate members.

Sometimes professionals are brought in to help and they can be struck by the dedication of its members—some who have never stepped on stage before. As stage director Debra Whitfield says, "I don't worry about their experience or lack of, I challenge them just as hard and I know everyone's giving me the best of their ability."

Since 1884 the Amateur Comedy Club has put on live performances continuously every year. There have been over 850 productions and counting.

The club was started by seven amateur actors wanting to break from the Madison Square Dramatic Organization so they could put performances which were more comedic in theme. Eventually the club would offer a mix of comedy, drama, and musicals through the years, putting on at least three major productions every year. Each production runs thirteen performances, mostly in a two-week period in the fall, winter, and spring. Sometimes there are also special live readings, cabaret, and social events.

Tradition runs deep for a club this old. Coat and tie are required for all men attending the shows. On Friday and Saturday, a formal tux must be worn. The only way to get

a ticket is through a member. Tickets are free with the only exception made during World War I when the club put on shows for the entertainment of U.S. Soldiers. Another club tradition: during intermission, show attendees are provided with free coffee and ice water. When The Snarks are in house it is traditionally lemonade.

The club has been located in its two now landmarked carriage houses since 1918. Every nook and cranny has been utilized for the immense work involved in putting on productions.

On the ground floor is the stage area which can seat up to 115 people. The tight space can be altered in a variety of ways to fit the productions. For instance for the play *Twelve Angry Men*, the audience was put in a theatre-in-the-round to mimic a courtroom setting.

Upstairs is the kitchen, green room, dressing rooms, and workroom. The green room is used during the intermission periods and contains a wonderful amount club memorabilia including every playbill of every production ever put on. There are also whimsical caricature drawings of past club members by renowned maritime artist, Gordon Grant. The workroom is another tight squeeze for members and includes the

members personal lockers—some painted with lively decorations. Many are light-heartedly used to hold member's personal "hootch." This tradition dates back to prohibition time when liquor needed to be hidden away. Though times have changed a bit, there is still an old saying at the club, "You can leave your wallet anywhere, but don't leave your drink unattended."

Over the years the club has seen its share of well-known people. Noted past members include Christopher La Farge whose architecture firm helped design parts of the Cathedral of St. John the Divine in New York. Frederick and John Steinway, members of the piano manufacturing family, were also members. Oscar-nominated actress Julie Harris graced the Amateur Comedy Club's stage in 1946 playing *Essie* in the play *The Devil's Disciples*.

THE SNARKS

The Snarks all-women amateur theatre group was born out of the same traditions and desires as the Amateur Comedy Club. Although entirely different clubs, they both rely on each other for their productions and events. The Snarks members are often at the Amateur's comedy club performing, building sets, and gathering props and costumes.

The Snarks was founded in 1909 by seven young women looking for an outlet to perform on stage during in a time when such offers were scant.

Their name comes from the Lewis Carroll poem, *The Hunting of the Snark*. Not even Carroll really knew what exactly a snark is, looks like or how it behaves - befitting for Snarks members in 1909. The name gave the sense that they could be what they desired without being categorized.

Today the Snarks have a similar membership structure to the Amateur Comedy Club where prospective members are sponsored by current ones. They also, put on a variety of live events every year for the amusement and interest of its members and friends.

BROOKLYN BRIDGE CIVIL DEFENSE

In a city where space is of utmost value and change is constant, some places in New York City can remain untouched for decades. In March 2006, city workers were inspecting the Brooklyn Bridge for structural problems when they stumbled onto a literal time capsule—an accidental one, created initially out of fear, but also preparedness in one of America's most tense and uneasy times.

The workers were inspecting one of the several storage vaults built into the bridge when it was constructed between 1870-1883. Inside one of these vaults on the Manhattan side of the bridge was a large hoard of Cold War-era rations and supplies—boxes and boxes of supplies looking straight out of a civil defense shelter. Labels on some of the items leave little question the stark reality for what they were meant. Blankets labeled "For Use Only After Enemy Attack" and medical supplies including boxes of Dextran which was used for treating shock and other ailments. Also, there were large amounts of food supplies—perhaps in anticipation of extended periods of time underground. Provisions like water in drum barrels (which was now evaporated) and an estimated 350,000+ crackers in tins labeled "Civil Defense All Purpose Survival Crackers." (Some surmise the crackers may even still be edible.) Even more unsettling for many may be the fact the drum barrels are marked, "Reuse as a commode."

All of the items were most likely put there in the mid-twentieth century. Some of the supplies were marked chillingly enough with two different years: 1957, when the

buildings along Park Avenue. Families regularly stockpiled rations in case of attack and some more industrious, or perhaps more frightened ones even built backyard bomb shelters.

Although today we know the utter severity of a nuclear blast would make these shelters, rations, and duck-and-cover procedures of little consequence to our well-being, one should not look at the past with condescending eyes. It may be easy to look at these actions as "quaint" or useless, but we would be remiss in not acknowledging the more important value these precautions had when the nuclear threat was indeed very real. It made people feel safer by giving the impression the government was doing something and that people could have control of their own destinies.

As for the fifty-foot-tall storage vaults in the bridge, they themselves are no secret. These arched brick cavernous spaces were always part of the plan construction of the bridge. However, like the Chrysler Building, with its proposed solarium, and the Empire State Building, with its proposed airship mooring mast, the bridge vaults were supposed to have a loftier future. Architect John Roebling's initial plans were to lease the vaults for wine storage and other items. Plans were also made to use some of the vaults as a shopping arcade.

Soviet's Sputnik Satellite went into space and 1962, the year of the Cuban Missile Crisis.

During the height of the tensions between the Soviet Union and United States, stockpiles of supplies like these were not an unusual in major cities. Today "Fallout Shelter" signs can still be seen in schools, many government buildings and even in the basements of luxury apartment

Although for a time a few were opened briefly on the Brooklyn side for occasional art shows, safety reasons shut the public out. As for the Cold-War-Era rations, today the city is mum on whether they are still there. Except for a brief tour of the room for press in 2006, the area has been closed off the the public. The exact location of the store room has never been publicly disclosed. One can only hope they are left undisturbed for the next generation to fascinate and ponder.

BROOKLYN BRIDGE

To this day, the Brooklyn Bridge is considered one of the greatest engineering feats in American history. It was the first suspension bridge in the world of this scale, making it for the forefront for all the others to come. Almost 6,000 feet long, the Gothic-style bridge could boast for twenty years as being the world's longest bridge.

Designed by John Augustus Roebling, it took fourteen years to build at the cost of fifteen million dollars. Six-hundred workers were required to build it, with over 40 men including Roebling himself dying during construction. Roebling's foot was crushed; he developed an infection and later died.

Today the Brooklyn Bridge is still very much an important part of the city's infrastructure. The NYC Department of Transportation says over 120,000 vehicles, 4,000 pedestrians, and 3,100 bicyclists cross the bridge everyday.

BROOKLYN PARROTS

Look closely around the campus of Brooklyn College and one may catch flashes of bright green zipping through the air. High-pitched squawks and calls normally heard in a pet store or zoo are a further tip off something unusual is afoot. One has just wandered in the now indigenous habitat of what seems like an oxymoron: The wild parrots of Brooklyn.

These fascinating birds are a yet another example of immigrants, albeit feathery ones, adapting to the unpredictability and mayhem of New York City. Called monk parakeets or Quaker parrots, the birds have been spotted in The Bronx, Brooklyn, Queens and slivers of New Jersey and Long Island.

How they got here is shadowed in lore and mystery. The first published sighting was in 1967 stemming theoretically from a pet owner or pet shop escape. Their certainly more colorful legend has its beginnings at John F. Kennedy International Airport. Some say burglars, perhaps the even mobsters, were scrounging around for valuable shipments when broke into a shipping container from Argentina filled with the birds who then flew the coop.

Through the 1970s and 1980s the parrots were spotted ever more frequently. The city pinned them as invasive species and began quietly trying to eradicate the birds with traps and poison. Still the parrots thrived.

Adapting here is not surprising considering the similarities between the parrots' Argentinian homeland and New York City. For one, Argentina is about as far away

from the Equator south as New York City is north, thus giving both humid summers and plenty of snow in the winter. So just like human New Yorkers, the birds are adept at somewhat schizophrenic seasons. Also, the breed is very intelligent, resourceful, and adapts quickly to new environments. In a pinch, the parrots will eat acorns, pine needles, and bird seed. Something not lost on a few local bird lovers who slyly put out bird seed specifically for their parrot neighbors.

The parrots' unofficial ambassador is Brooklyn resident Steve Baldwin who offers free tours to the parrots' habitats. He only asks that attendees not reveal the nests' locations or disturb them. He says it is important to enlighten people, make them feel good about the birds, and therefore keep the public is on their side.

Steve became fascinated with them years ago, declaring them one of the best shows in town, "There's always some situation going on, they're always working. They are carefully putting together their nests, canoodling, standing guard, kind of like what people do on a brownstone stoop. You got one guy trying to work, two others are fighting—it's sort of a hullabaloo going on."

Just like New Yorkers, they are creative when it comes to living spaces. The birds build ingenious complex multi-level dwellings.

Often they prefer building nests near electrical transformers on top of utility poles

photo © Juliet Hanlon

due to the emanating heat. The wires also make good anchors for the nests. The lack of these poles in Manhattan is one of the reasons the parrots have not made a go there.

Nowadays the parrots can be also seen in parts of The Bronx, Queens and parts of New Jersey and Long Island. The largest colony is most likely at Brooklyn College with some forty to fifty birds. The school has a live-and-let-live approach, carefully not disturbing their nests and mindful of their space when campus maintenance is necessary.

As for past worries the parrots would become an invasive species—except for occasionally bullying a squirrel for an acorn or muscling in on bird feeders, they too have a live-and-let-live credo.

Steve says after all these years the parrots are like the rest of us, having proved their mettle and taking what the city throws at them. "They're survivors. I saw one hit by a car, he sort shook his head and took off. They're like us they don't get fazed much."

He adds, "The parrots are just another weird, wonderful, special thing about New York City, which is a cornucopia of experiences and this is one."

And lest we forget—with all the talk about WILD parrots, many should actually consider keeping some as a pet. They are wonderful, loyal birds and Steve points to the 1970s craze where Argentina couldn't send enough over here for pet owners. There are parrot rescue agencies all over the internet to help potential adopters. Just don't think of plucking one out of the wild! For you and the bird's sake, it's about as smart as taking in a feral cat.

GREEN-WOOD CEMETERY

One of the spots in New York City that the monk parrots seem to find particularly hospitable is Green-Wood Cemetery in Brooklyn. This historic cemetery opened in 1840 and is a bit more bucolic than the wilds of Brooklyn College. The parrots seem to relish building their nests in cemetery's grand northern entrance arch.

Some of the more notable people interred here include Samuel F. B. Morris, Peter Cooper, Leonard Bernstein, and several members of President Theodore Roosevelt's family.

As for Green-Wood Cemetery, they too are trying to take a live and let live approach with the parrots. At times they can be a problem when it comes to their taking over some of the more fragile parts of the stone edifies, but the caretakers try to accommodate the birds as much as possible.

BURGER JOINT

In a city that over-intellectualizes everything from fine wine to pizza, the classic all-American burger is now in New Yorkers' crosshairs. But the overall consensus is the burger joint gets it spectacularly right, with a twist; classic eats hidden in plain sight.

To find to the burger joint (yes, lowercase), one must first traipse through the five star Le Parker Meridien hotel lobby—an expansive contemporary space; a bit "intimidating" but certainly not out of place for Midtown Manhattan. To the uninitiated, this might seem like a fool's journey for burgers, but with a little patience they can be found.

Concierges and bellhops will wait a moment before helping people looking for burger joint, but will give a bemused smile which seemingly says, "Yes, you're on the right track."

Off to the Northwest side of the lobby is an enormous, floor-to-ceiling curtain. Peek around the corner—and a wordless neon burger sign beacons that this is the spot.

Then almost like stepping onto a movie set, one's world is transformed immediately from swanky big city hotel, to a small town eatery. Some say the vibe reminds them of a local college hangout. Wood tables and booths are first come first serve. Wall paneling is dressed with graffiti and posters. The velvet curtain has done its second duty well: masking the smells of grilling burgers that are now enveloping one's nose.

The burger joint is the brainchild of restauranteur Steven Pipes and Le Parker Meridien's executive chef Emile Castillo.

Started back "On a lark," according to Stephen in 2002, it has proven to be not just

a gimmick. The place has serious food credentials. Several foodie outlets put its burgers in the top five for the city. Proof alone is the healthy mix of tourists and businesspeople there during lunch hour. The line often snakes outside the curtain (sometimes ruining the treasure hunt).

The menu is short. Burgers can be ordered single or double. Along with a side of extra crispy fries or a pickle.

Pitchers of beer and shakes help wash down the meal and there are brownies that deserve their own "joint."

As for the burgers, Pipes and Castillo settled on one burger recipe after dozens of testings and tastings. They discovered that reinventing the wheel was not necessary. The burgers are simple are a cut above.

Five-ounce patties are ground fresh in-house using top quality meat. Meat is put once through a "hand grinder giving it a course grind." Castillo says, "The meat is touched little as possible because it hardens the burger."

As for any special sauce or spices: look elsewhere; not even salt is added. Castillo says it, "covers up the quality of the meat and can dry it out."

Burgers are cooked and assembled on demand: rare, medium, or well on a toasted bun. "A gas grill is used so a burger is not allowed to cook in its own fat. Rather the fat falls through onto the briquette, and that adds flavor to the burger." It is as close to a backyard barbecue taste anyone is going to get in the middle of Manhattan.

Burgers are dressed with classic add-ons like ketchup, Dijon mustard, mayonnaise, lettuce, tomatoes, pickles, onions, or the catch-all, "The Works."

Of course there is a hardy offering of cheese, if so desired, Castillo settled on white cheddar and Colby for the best blend in terms of melting and taste.

All of this burger magic is done right before your eyes in a tiny kitchen behind the counter. Logistics demand speed and synchronicity as orders loom from the ever growing lunch hour crowd.

The close quarters has had at least one positive consequence—two of the kitchen staff met here and eventually married.

Success here has also spanned two other Burger Joint branches in the city with more conventional storefronts. Perhaps with less mystique but at least they lessen the load for the "worst secret in town" —Le Parker Meridien's Burger Joint.

HAMBURGERS

Like many other "All-American" foods, the hamburger most likely came here by way of immigrants. It is largely thought the hamburgers derived from Hamburg steaks in Germany in the 19th Century. However they did not really become popular in America until they were served at the World's Fair in Saint Louis, Missouri in 1904.

During World War I they were referred to as "Liberty sandwiches" to avoid the German reference. It is estimated Americans eat 50 billion burgers every year accounting for seventy-one percent of all the beef consumed at American eateries and sixty percent of all sandwiches.

BYWAYS AND SKYWAYS

The sheer number of people in New York City makes for some interesting and creative ways to get from point to point. Every New Yorker has their own personal shortcuts, passageways and unconventional routes they swear by. But one of the most visual and intriguing are the aerial bridges running through the skyline. Though many have long put out of commission, they still hold the public's imagination.

Skyways make sense. Instead of going all the way down a building then all the way up another, one is not only avoiding messy pedestrian traffic and weather but efficiently moving building to building.

Case in point is the old Gimbels Skybridge in Herald Square. Though the department store is long gone, the bridge still strikes a dramatic pose in an otherwise now garish part of the city. At one time Gimbels was in a head-to-head fight with Macy's to be the world's biggest and best department store. In the early part of the 20th century, both were quickly expanding, taking over as much Midtown Manhattan space as they could. Gimbels was eagerly wanted a presence on more coveted Fifth Avenue, so it took over nearby Cuyer Building on 32nd Street, joining the buildings with the skybridge.

It was built in 1925 by the architectural firm Shreve and Lamb, who would go on to design the Empire State Building. As for the skybridge, this three-story art deco master-piece, sheathed in copper juts out of the now defunct department store. With its broad open windows looking out to the city, surely it was a ploy to get customers into the building. In 1995 the skybridge was slated for demolition, but was seemingly saved because of the high cost of demolition.

METROPOLITAN LIFE BUILDINGS

On 24th Street between Madison and Park Avenue is the shiny aluminum clad skyway linking the Metropolitan Life North Build-ing to the Met Life Tower. The design was inspired by the skybridge at St. Marks Campanile in Venice Italy. Met Life left the buildings in 2005 and now Credit Suisse occupies the space. The skybridge could see some interesting uses in the future for the upper floors of the tower are being turned into hotel rooms.

GRAND CENTRAL SKYWAY

Though indoors, perhaps the most spectac-ular skybridge view in the city is at Grand Central Terminal. The bridge spans across the famous windows of the terminal on both sides. The high view offers a panoramic view of the terminal few ever see. Even the floor is transparent giving pedestrians an almost walk along the heavens feel, especially if one looks just above for they are just feet away for the Terminal's constellations mural on the ceiling. Incredibly, the top arches have small windows that open outward giving a complete and unobtrusive view of Grand Central.

CHINESE SCHOLAR'S GARDEN

Who would have thought of all places, Staten Island to be home one of only two Chinese scholar's gardens in the United States-- not to begrudge the borough of this distinction, but after visiting the garden, many will wonder why there are not others. Located in the Staten Island Botanical Garden at the Snug Harbor Cultural Center, the garden offers a quiet repose in an authentic setting rarely experienced out of China.

Chinese scholar's gardens were first created during China's Ming Dynasty for retiring scholars and administrators of the Emperor's court. The gardens are made up of natural elements--rocks, wood, water, and plants--which are placed in a deliberate and symbolic manner. The goal is to create an environment with a visual order and harmony where visitors find tranquility and a place for quiet contemplation.

Just like those in China, the New York Chinese Scholar's Garden has various elements symbolizing several traditional themes and concepts. They include a koi pond, bamboo field, waterfalls, a rockery, and eight pavilions with several covered walkways. Many of the materials and artisans who created the garden came from Suzhou, China which is well known for its private gardens and mastery of the art. No nails or glue are used in the construction of the wood elements, rather they are joined together using traditional Chinese skills and artistry.

The garden is actually made up of twenty smaller gardens with various themes. For instance rocks are thought of as being the bones of the earth, water are the arteries of the world, furniture are the internal organs and paintings and calligraphy symbolize the knowledge of art and literature of the garden's owner.

The buildings also play a central role in the gardens for they are integrated in harmony with natural elements. Doorways are more than entry points. They frame areas inside the garden, providing infinite angles of viewpoints. Walls are put in strategic places to maximize design elements, as are walkways so the gardens can be enjoyed at different views and angles. Bridges called one-steps are also manipulated to curve severely so different viewpoints can be enjoyed. They also use small steps on the bridge to cause visitors to walk slowly, thus giving them time to take and contemplate the surroundings.

So how did a Chinese scholar's garden end up in Staten Island? It was the idea of then Staten Island Botanical Garden President Frances Paulo Huber who in 1984 felt a garden like this would be enjoyed and cherished by the community. Despite being a bit off the beaten track for most New Yorkers, many people still make their way her. Some marvel at the workmanship, others find a quiet corner to read or think. Wedding and other photo shoots are also common. Even though it's a world away from it provenance, there is nothing lost in translation when it comes to the peace and serenity the garden gives to everyone.

CITY HALL STATION

Beautiful and elegant are words not normally used when speaking about a subway station. But then again, until recently, few have seen or even heard of the now defunct City Hall subway station in Lower Manhattan.

It was built as a showcase station to illustrate what could be achieved by a city that was on the move and growing.

The station opened in 1904, a time when New York City was becoming a city of the world. Just a few years before in 1898, all five boroughs had incorporated to become one giant municipality. Brooklyn alone was already the second largest city in the country behind New York City. It was a time for the new metropolis to think big, roll the dice, and pronounce itself ready for its next era. Part of the equation meant having a mass transit better than any other city and it was the City Hall station job that set the tone.

Architects George Lewis Heins and Christopher Grant Lafarge were assigned to the task by the Interborough Rapid Transit Company in 1900 to build what would be the southern terminal of the first New York City subway line. The two were already gaining fame for their design of the city's Cathedral of St. John the Divine. Cathedral influences are apparent inside the station. Vaulted tiled arches are everywhere and there is not a straight line in sight. Hints of Romanesque Revival pepper the space. The Guastavino terra cotta tiled ceilings and skylights made of amethyst give the underground space an ornate and graceful feel.

Even today, the City Hall station's influences are present throughout the New York City subway system. For example the tell-tale mosaic tiles seen in many stations were first used here.

Opening day for station, on October 27, 1904 was a grand affair. Mayor George B. McClellan steered the first train with a special silver handle made by Tiffany & Co. Some 15,000 passes were given out—upwards of 150,000 people were veering for a spot to try out the new subway system.

City Hall station's life was a bit short-lived thanks in part to the success of the rapid subway expansion spreading its railway tentacles quickly across the city. More stations meant more passengers and train cars. The longer trains required could not fit on the City Hall's relatively short and curved platform. And with the Brooklyn Bridge Subway Station being so close by, City Hall station was fast becoming obsolete. For years the station was even closed at night. In fact by 1945, its last year of operation, only around 600 people actually used it.

Fortunately after it closed, City Hall Station was somewhat forgotten but left intact. It became landmarked 1979 and ideas to reuse the space were always mulled around. Slowly the station was restored and cleaned.

Unfortunately because of security and safety concerns, the station is limited to exclusive tours. To apply for a tour one must become a member of the New York City Transit Museum and a few times a year the museum offers tickets for the tour online on a first come, first serve basis. They often sell out 20 minutes after they are posted. Too bad, for this is a space not only New Yorkers should revere, but also be proud of.

COLUMBIA NUCLEAR REACTOR

It sounds like one of those urban legends or perhaps a tall tale that college upperclassmen utter to gullible freshmen, but it is indeed true: Columbia University has its own nuclear reactor. Though it has never been used and is now permanently mothballed, the reactor is located in the Engineering Terrace building on the university's Morningside Heights campus.

To 21st century minds, this might seem absurd, but schools acquiring their own nuclear reactors is not as unbelievable considering time and context. During the early 1960s a number of universities and research facilities wanted reactors for various educational and research purposes. Moreover, these were not the kind of nuclear reactors used in power plants, rather 250 KW reactors which were a fraction of the size.

It was a time when nuclear technology was being carefully exploited to see just what benefits there were to be had in everything from energy efficiency to medical research. With the Cold War brewing, nuclear science was an important discipline for both the United States and Soviet Union.

In 1960, Columbia University was awarded a quarter-of-a-million-dollar grant from the National Science Foundation to install a nuclear reactor. The university was already a pioneer of nuclear technology. In 1939, Columbia scientists proved nuclear fission was possible with uranium and could make an explosion. Furthermore, initial research for The Manhattan Project which led to the creation of the atomic bomb was done inside a particle accelerator on campus.

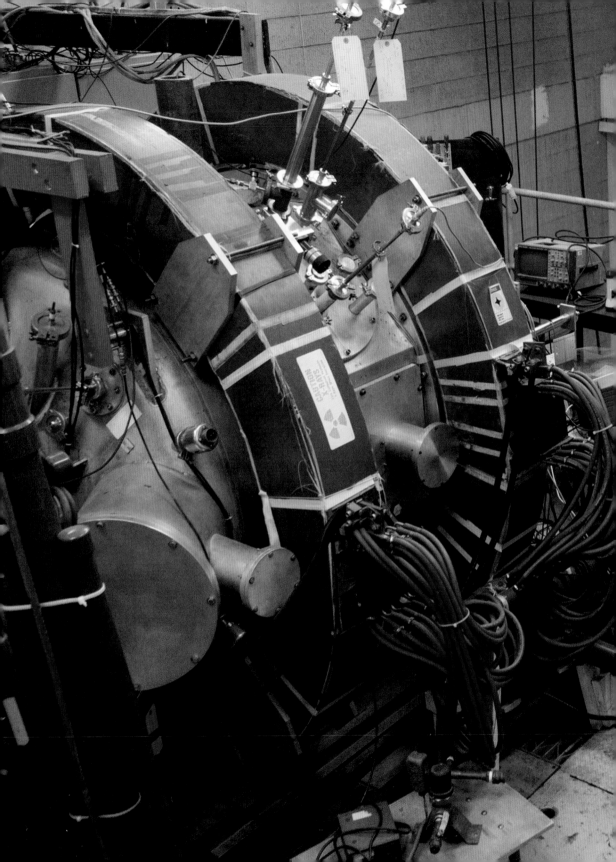

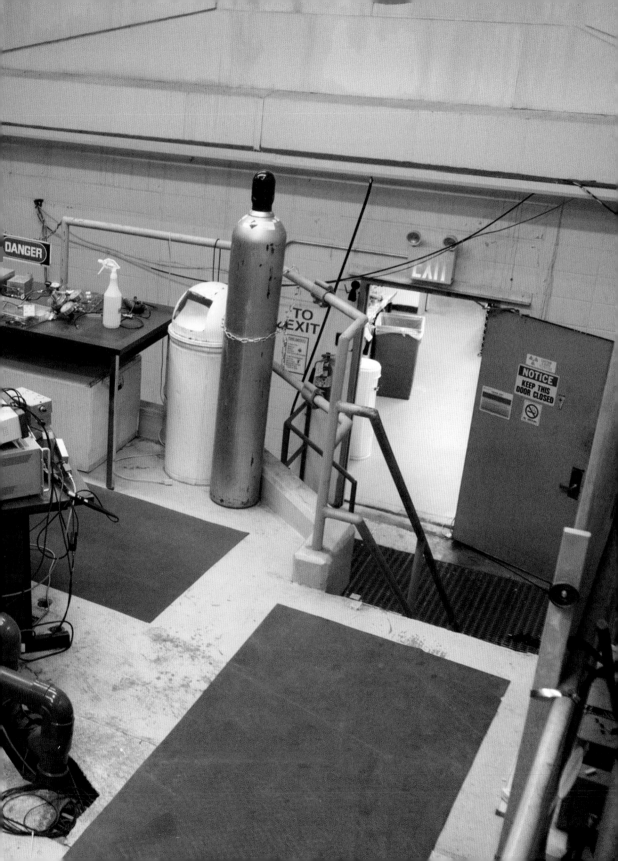

As for the nuclear reactor, when it was finished in 1967 it cost one million dollars. It was all for naught, it was never even tested or loaded with any kind of radioactive material.

The year 1968 was a turbulent time for Columbia University. The campus saw numerous demonstrations against the school for their involvement with the U.S. Government in the Vietnam War. So with feelings and emotions already running high, the increasing fear and anxiety about nuclear power and students already petitioning against the reactor, the university delayed their application from the Atomic Energy Commission for a operating license.

They reapplied in 1969 and were issued one in 1971. But in 1972, protestors filed a petition in the U.S. Court of Appeals to review the decision which had been denied. It went to the Supreme Court which upheld Columbia's right to the license. However by this time it was 1974 and the university was reevaluating its entire Nuclear Science and Engineering program, so the project was put on indefinite hold due partly because of budget and management concerns. Then in 1979 just months after the Three Mile Island nuclear reactor accident in Pennsylvania, the university permanently withdrew their request for a license. Then university president Dr. William J. McGill even declared the

reactor would never be activated while he was in charge. That pretty much sealed the reactor's fate.

Today, it still sits where it was built, looking like not much more than a giant three tiered concrete block. Some of the original remnants are still there like the ceiling crane and and a few gauges here and there. As for the inside, some of the parts are still intact, but unusable due to rust and time. Just like any other piece of manufactured equipment or appliance, the reactor has a nameplate reading, "TRIGA MARK II."

Fuel rods would have been inserted from the floor above, but it has been sealed up. However, one can still walk over the steel grating where the rods would have sat in an open pool of water; common for this kind of reactor, because water is excellent at keeping the core cool and safe.

As for why the reactor is still here? Practicality or lack of it. Dr. Michael Mauel, Professor of Applied Physics at Columbia University says, "Removing the epoxy-lined cement walls is just too much work and expense. So we work around it."

So with space at a premium like everywhere else in New York City, Mauel and his students are using the abandoned reactor hall for physics experiments and storage. Surrounding the reactor are a hodgepodge of scientific equipment too specialized and

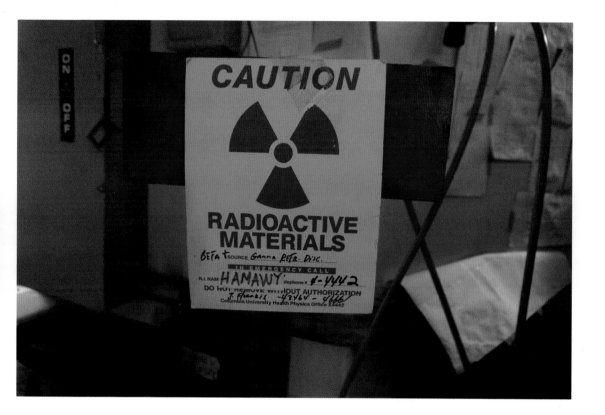

unique to throw out, so parts wait patiently for their next use. Somewhat fittingly on top of the actual reactor is an experimental plasma vessel for creating space weather experiments and advancing how strong magnetic force fields confine ionized matter heated to 100 million degrees for fusion energy. Professor Mauel says, "That's really the next step for nuclear power." These particular experiments allow students and scientists to create and control gases heated to temperatures higher than found in the sun and better understand the environment found in outer-space.

As the reactor sits idle, first because of politics, now changing research needs, it is nothing more than a bench used for experiments for the next era of research. As George Hamawy, retired radiation safety officer at Columbia University wrote in the Radiation Safety Journal in May 2002, "It serves as a reminder of another era when scientific dreams were placed on hold because of the social and financial realities of the time."

DEAD HORSE BAY

No one by any means is looking towards this stretch of beach for a romantic or contemplative stroll. Frankly describing it as post-apocalyptic, polluted and filthy is being kind. But this small stretch of beach on the outer edges of Brooklyn, draws a bevy of different people. Be it history buffs, scavengers, artists, crafters or just the curious, they are all are drawn to Dead Horse Bay—the inlet time forgot.

This half mile or so of beach on a lonesome cove is strewed with countless bits trash from little bits of ceramics to large unrecognizable chunks of twisted metal. For over 300 years, this tidal marsh area in Southwest Brooklyn never had a chance against human civilization. Since the 1600s, it is a place man has done his dirty business.

Settlement of the inlet began somewhat innocently enough when Dutch settlers used the tide waters here, which was once known as Barren Island to run their mills to process wheat. One of the age-old stone millstones is even today still resting in the marsh.

Next came the fish oil factories which harvested local menhaden fish from the shores; a messy, smelly process, fish oil was used for a variety of uses including the manufacturing of soap, candles and tanning.

In the 1850s the island's distance from the rest of the local population, made it a prudent place for the unpleasant practice of horse rendering. When horses or other

domesticated animals were no longer of use or had died, they were sent here for their final function. The animal carcusses were boiled, processed, then made into glue, soap, and fertilizer among other products. The process gave off a putrid smell intolerable to even the most heartiest of stomachs.

Adding to the mess were garbage incinerators burning trash from Brooklyn and Manhattan, which together must have seemed like hell on earth. Incredibly, the men who worked there and their families called this place "home" despite no sewage or water systems and only being accessible by boat. There was even a local school house for the children and, of course, a most welcomed necessity for the men—a saloon.

Dead Horse Bay got a reprieve from its noxious uses thanks in part to the advent of the automobile. With horses no longer a necessary form of transportation, the rendering plants closed down. By the 1920s only one still existed of the more than two dozen rendering plants that once dotted the shoreline.

In 1926, most of the marsh and Barren Island was filled in with more garbage and sand and landfill so the city's first municipal airport, Floyd Bennett Field could be built nearby.

Even more landfill occurred in the 1950s when New York City unloaded more of its waste and refuse here—much of it from buildings demolished to make way for public infrastructure and housing. Soon the landfill was at capacity, and it was covered over or "capped." However erosion and the sheer mass of refuse quickly caused the contents of the landfill to spill out, forever creeping out of its sandy grave.

Today this old landfill, and long forgotten industrial waterfront, is revealing itself one tide at a time, much to the delight of curiosity seekers. It provides a fascinating glimpse into the past lives of others.

One cannot help but be an amateur archeologist while strolling the beach. Fragments and bits of materials cause one to stop and wonder. It might be a curiously shaped bottle that makes one ponder what contents it may have held,. (And why are there so many Clorox bottles?)

The vast majority of refuse is glass. During low tide the water gently cascades over glass items creating an eerie tinkling sound. At sunset, glass fragments embedded on the beach glisten in the sun rays creating a befuddling beautiful sight.

Peppered among the glass are large

twisted bits of metal and aluminum. Shoe soles and white walled tires are also common. There too is a smattering of a bone fragments from the former island's horse rendering days. Off the shoreline is the still capped area of the landfill waiting for its turn for erosion to peel away its layers. Already bits of paper and other fragile items reveal themselves from the side of the beach berm.

One particular item on the beach which is seemingly indestructible are thousands of women's nylon stockings. They congregate in bizarre looking tangled up globs grounded by the sands captured in their mesh.

One positive realization one can gleam from all this trash: nary a piece of plastic is to be found. Somehow it has yet to wash up and take a foothold on the beach.

On any given day the beach has people with bags collecting their own samples. It is interesting what strikes an individual's particular fancy here; none of it is particularly worth anything, but, as the old adage goes, one man's trash is another man's treasure. People picking through the bits and pieces fixate on items that others ignore. Some are looking for colored bits of glass for art projects, while others take items home to look them up on the internet and identify them out of sheer curiosity.

This brings up an interesting dilemma. Since the stretch of land is now under the Jamaica Unit of the Gateway National Recreation Area and under National Park Service jurisdiction, technically it is illegal to take anything off the land. But many constitute this as what is it—trash—and needs to be cleaned up. Either way the Park Service is actively looking to stop the erosion and stop the spillage. So do they leave the trash as part of a piece of history or as a window into our past, or is it a hazardous site?

Either way with the tides, the surface is always revealing something new that is old to its visitors.

FLOYD BENNET FIELD

Right across the road from Dead Horse Bay is a former airport which has seen its share of history.

Not many realize the former Floyd Bennett Field was the first municipal airport in New York City and which has had its share of VIP's and aviation firsts.

Opened in 1930, it was merely a dirt runway with just one pilot giving short sightseeing flights. But because the field was free of any obstructions easy for pilots to see from the sky, the airport grew in use. Millions of cubic yards of sand were brought in to expand what was then Barren Island and to create a full scale airport.

Passenger facilities were built, with the verve and gusto—albeit smaller scale of Grand Central Terminal and Penn Station. The main building was an Art Deco gem using designs congruent with modern air travel.

Unfortunately, with the Great Depression looming and Americans still a bit apprehensive about air travel, the airport was never a large scale commercial passenger enterprise.

However, the airport had its share of significant and historic events. Famed aviators Amelia Earnhart, Wiley Post, Howard Hughes, and Roscoe Turner all used the field to break world record flights. Even Douglas "Wrong Way" Corrigan made his "accidental" flight to Ireland instead of California from here.

Over the years however the long trek to South Brooklyn proved too much for many New Yorkers. The airfield was eventually appropriated to the U. S. military until it was deactivated in 1971.

The good news is the National Park Service has acquired it now as part of the Gateway National Recreation Area. It is a great place for birding and hiking with several trails on and off the runways. Even the main terminal building has been restored to its original glory with exhibits on the history of the airport.

ECLECTIC/ENCORE PROPS

Eclectic/Encore Props is one of the largest prop companies on the East Coast. Owned by founder and president Suri Bieler, the company rents props for movies, television, and even special events like weddings and corporate parties. Curiously, live theatre particularly Broadway shows are not regular clients. Suri says one of the reasons involves a bit of a superstition. For in the theatre world, the hope is a new production will last for years. So it is considered bad luck to use something in a show that has to be returned on a deadline (therefore one is jinxing the production).

As for inventory, Eclectic Props has a selection of over one million props and counting. Most are displayed in a Long Island City, Queens warehouse—a former bottling plant for Pepsi-Cola. The company moved there not only because their Manhattan location was quickly running out of space, but also because Long Island City has become the de facto movie center of New York City. Major studios Silvercup and Kaufmann-Astoria Studios are right in their backyard.

Their 95,000 square foot Eclectic's warehouse almost looks like a bizarre department store filled with vintage and wide-ranging items meticulously inventoried and cared for.

Each floor is sectioned off in different rooms with particular "themes." It is like every corner is like stepping into another era, country, or way of life. For example there is the Medical Room full of health-care-related items like medicine jars, wheelchairs, surgical instruments, and other various medical equipment There are world theme sections like the Morocco or the Asia areas filled with similarly themed furniture, assorted knick-knacks, and objects. One of the favorites is the "old New York" section, complete with old time Yiddish store signs, and cityscape decor like a newsstand and phone booth. Period furniture is also categorized to match the theme and time period that productions are looking for. Ranging from Louis XVI to mid-century and beyond.

Throughout the day, Suri can be seen going floor to floor helping production designers find just the right prop for their production. She understands the challenge, but for most of us, a chair is often just a chair—an innocuous object serving little purpose to the production.

But as Suri explains, props do not just match a time period, but more importantly they match the character and theme of the

scene. Suri says, "Props can often cue the viewer into what is going on in a scene." It is also important the furniture not only matches the scene, but more importantly the character. Props are not just conveying a time frame of the scene, but can also reveal the personality of the actors and context of the scene."

With all these particular and specific props, incredibly everything at Eclectic Props is available online for inspection and rental. Still, set designers come here daily to peruse the items not only looking for specific items but to spur on ideas for themes.

For a set designer looking for "just the right piece," it is like mining gold.

Suri kind of fell into her business by happenstance. In the 1980s she was working for a set designer for a movie and was asked to find a stuffed deer head. Flummoxed on where to find it in the middle of Manhattan, she was directed to a prop rental company. The visit was one of those "ah-ha" moments for her, giving her the idea to start her own company.

With just $175 she began acquiring items, even accumulated them from off the street where she says she has found some

of the best items. She also began buying items from finished Broadway theatre productions and the rest is history.

Today, many people will just email her with cool stuff.

Before you begin to have visions of starting your own prop company, you should know there is a method to acquiring these items. Eclectic acquires specialized items, often hard-to-find period pieces, and commercial grade objects.

And because of the industrial feel of their facilities, their rooftop views and the convenience, Eclectic Props also rents their spaces for film and fashion shoots. They can even design sets for clients.

With all the visual delights in their spaces, they have had requests for the public just to have a "look around." Luckily for us, Suri says she is looking into allowing tours through the facilities in the near future.

NY MOVIES

Over the last twenty years the movie business in New York City has become an industry to reckoned with; contributing some 8.7 billion dollars and over 130,000 jobs to the local economy. In a way this is not surprising considering some of the very first motion pictures ever were filmed in Manhattan.

ELLIS ISLAND OFF LIMITS

The Statue of Liberty and Ellis Island are not only symbolic but are also a literal gateway and beacon for some twelve and a half million immigrants from 1892 to 1954. It is no wonder year after year the ancestors of many of these immigrants make a pilgrimage here, to one of the most visited historical sites in all of the United States.

But as popular as the Main Building at Ellis Island and Statue of Liberty are, there is a part of the Island few see: equally fascinating and perhaps even more poignant.

It is simply known as the South Side—a building complex which for many immigrants, was a place skirted between hope and heartbreak.

Immigrants could be denied entry for a number of reasons. If they were suspected of being a law breaker, political radical, or of having contract work waiting for them on arrival they might be sent back. Others could be deemed too sick to enter the country. And with one in ten immigrants needing some sort of medical care after their perilous boat trip to America, it was a sobering concern.

During an entry interview, if immigration officers suspected someone was not within the guidelines, their clothing was marked with a chalk symbol. For example, "X" meant mental defect and "C" was for conjunctivitis. Being pregnant ("PG") could even earn a mark.

Many of those marked were taken to the South Side complex until their illness subsided, and/or they were well enough to return to their homeland, and/or they had made arrangements to go back to their homeland. They could also request a hearing to plead their case.

Along with administrative offices, the South Side included two hospitals, staff housing, a morgue, kitchen, laundry rooms and the staff's house.

Rules could be heart-wrenching. Sometimes if one family member was ill, the whole family had to return to their homeland. But in the end, ninety percent of all who entered the hospital managed to improve and enter the United States.

Ironically many of the detainees received better medical treatment here than they did in their home country. Ellis Island's hospital was state of the art and included such innovations as fluoroscopy equipment and an autoclave machine to sterilize whole mattresses (it can still be seen in the hospital today).

Another innovation was a series of enclosed corridors throughout the main hospital, done so to section off infectious diseases wards as well as keep patients away from the elements.

Today, much of the South Side Complex is in a state of "arrested decay." Save Ellis Island, the non-profit partner of the National Park Service is currently working to raise the necessary funds to preserve and restore the hospital complex. The result is quite unforgettable and strangely beautiful. For instance at the staff's house, the worn but still colorful paint and rough wood strike a dramatic tone as the bay winds blow through blown out windows. The stirring site is a reminder of how exposed Ellis Island is to the natural elements.

There is also an intimacy one feels to those of the past here. Though the current decay is not representative of the past, restorations and cleanups have not scrubbed away the minor details. It is not whitewashed, rather raw and pure. Small human touches can be found, like pencilled graffiti probably put there by someone biding their time until they got better. Mundane laundry and kitchen equipment, though not very picturesque, is left in place putting things into correct context.

Some items, though innocuous at first sight, offer stark realities of living here. Like the patient's rooms that include two sinks—one for cleaning, the other for draining the nose and throat because of the dreaded Tuberculosis disease. Then there is the morbid—and antiseptic morgue complete with iceboxes for the dead.

During World War II, Ellis Island, like many institutions, took on new responsibilities. For a time it held foreign national detainees. Some 7,000 Germans, Italians, and Japanese would wait the war out. Many were employed here lending a hand in maintenance and kitchen work. The island also housed injured soldiers just returning from

ELLIS ISLAND

Ellis Island is one of the most popular historical destinations in America with some three million people visit it every year. Not much of a surprise considering an estimated forty percent of Americans can trace their ancestors coming through Ellis Island.

Its biggest year in terms of immigration came in 1907 when just over one million being processed into the country. Most of them would have been processed in the Registry Room; i.e. today's Main Building. Over the years it was often referred informally as the "Great Hall" because of its enormous space. It is indeed, but for many immigrants it was the largest area indoors they had ever seen, thus inspiring to it to be referred to as "Great."

Today visitors can search through Ellis Island's registry and find their ancestor's records. The museum even offers a facsimile copy of the logbook showing your family's entry.

the front and for a time was a training station for the U.S. Coast Guard.

In 1954, Ellis Island processed its last immigrant. Soon afterward it was abandoned and rapidly deteriorated. But by 1965 it was incorporated into the Statue of Liberty National Monument and listed on

the National Register of Historic Places the following year. The Great Hall reopened in 1990 to great fanfare after a massive restoration. Today it is a museum housing exhibit and performance spaces.

As for South Side complex, visitors can now see it for themselves on a special "Hard Hat" guided tour led by Save Ellis Island Docents. Because of logistics, the tours are very limited in size. "Save Ellis Island" knows the importance of the South Side as they plan to rehabilitate portions of the complex and while trying to make more tours available.

EXPLORER'S CLUB

Visiting the Explorer's Club on East 70th Street is not unlike an adventure onto itself. The Club began in 1904 for adventure minded individuals to have a place to research, support and discuss expeditions to the ends of the earth. This was during the era of grand exploration where mankind was testing its limits into unknown and inhospitable lands. Executive Director Will Roseman says, "This was the time when the Arctic explorer were the rock stars of their time." Newspapers of the day scrambled to print the up to date details from dispatches of the latest expeditions around the earth.

Members of the Explorer's Club have been on many of the greatest expeditions in history, including the first expeditions to the North and South Poles, the first to the top of Mount Everest, many moon landings and as well as the lowest ocean depth.

As one of the oldest clubs in New York City, it has managed to survive thanks to its dedication of active learning and discovery. This is not a shrine, rather an active place where decades of members and their exploits have enriched the club with a plethora of information, individuals, and artifacts.

Just strolling through the multi-floor former mansion is a lesson in history of human exploration. Seemingly every nook and cranny has one great artifact or memento after another rivaling the best museums. There are animal pelts and bones, ancient pieces

from archeological digs, and equipment used on some of the greatest expeditions around the world and beyond.

Tradition has provided the Explorer's Club lots of artifacts, for it was considered good form for members to bring back something from their exhibition for the club. Like the skin of a tiger said to have killed nine men in Africa. There is also Robert Perry's sled used during his exposition to the north pole. In the front waiting room, sits a coffee table made from a hatch from the USS *Explorer*. This research ship was one of only seven ships to survive Pearl Harbor. Upstairs is another table, this one used by President Theodore Roosevelt during his cabinet meetings. He said to have used it while drumming up plans with engineers for the Panama Canal. One of the more, shall we say, interesting and surprisingly intriguing items is a penis of a sperm whale mounted on a handsomely carved wooden base.

Even the club's building has a storied past. The Jacobean-style mansion was built by Stephen C. Clark one of the heirs of the Singer Sewing Machine family fortune. Clark was an avid art collector and used authentic Renaissance pieces in the construction of the home. From that era is an intricately carved marble fireplace and an outdoor colonnade on the patio originally from a French monastery. Finely carved wood panelling and moulding from the 1500s adorn the first floor.

The building is well used, for the club regularly hosts symposiums and special events featuring an array of specialists and scientists sharing their research and exploits.

One of the more "colorful" events is their annual dinner to honor individual explorers. The menu is not for the faint of heart. Items have included Madagascar hissing cockroaches, martinis with goats eyes, and scorpions with endive. Main courses have included muskrat, alligator, beaver, and ostrich. The idea behind such peculiar offerings is to illustrate what can be considered edible on other sides of the earth.

Another club tradition is to carry the Explorer's Club official flag on an expedition. Variations of the flag have been carried on hundreds of trips including four Apollo missions, several trips to both poles including the first solo North Pole expedition by Naomi Uemura. One particular flag, Number 161 has been have been to the highest point of the world (Mount Everest) and the lowest point in the world (Challenger Deep) which was taken by filmmaker James Cameron on his Deepsea Challenger Expedition. The Challenger Deep is a underwater trench in the Pacific Ocean near Mariana Island thought to be the deepest point on the earth's surface.

Members of the Explorer's Club are a who's who of exploration and the pursuit of knowledge. They include Sir Edmund Hillary, Neil Armstrong, Charles Lindbergh and Robert Peary. More recent members include underwater archaeologist and Titanic discoverer Robert Ballard, Amazon co-founder Jeff Bezos, and Tesla Motors founder Elon Musk, whose venture SpaceX is heralding a new phase of space travel. Honorary members include Theodore Roosevelt, the Duke of Edinburgh, and Walter Cronkite.

But do not think just climbing something like Mount Everest gives one automatic membership into the club. "K2 perhaps, but not Mount Everest," muses Will. Though there are 3,000 members, getting in requires extensive previous travel and recommendations from several members.

But luckily for the public or mere weekend explorers, the Explorers Club is one of the city's best kept secret when it comes to events open to the public and are always open to helping others with their extensive archive of books, journals, and manuscripts. They often have some events open to the public as well as tours of the building.

ROY CHAPMAN ANDREWS

One of the more intriguing curios at the Explorer's Club is a leather whip once owned by Roy Chapman Andrews. He is not necessarily a household name, but most of us are familiar with his exploits in a roundabout way. A former president of the Explorer's club himself and director of the American Museum of Natural History, Andrews was an explorer and naturalist who specialized in expeditions in China, the Gobi Desert, and Mongolia. Andrews' writings about his personal exploits made him quite famous for his time. Those tales were said to be the basis of the fictional character Indiana Jones, though it has never been confirmed by the character's creators. As for the whip, at one particular event, someone requested to hold it—none other than movie maker George Lucas.

FDR TRAIN

Second to only Times Square as the most visited place in New York City, Grand Central Terminal has been a gateway into the city for millions of people. There are over forty train platforms at Grand Central, but a little known, off-limits one known as "Platform 61" has also seen its share of visiting dignitaries, world leaders and celebrities. Its exact location is held secret by the Metropolitan Transit Authority. And for good reason, for today it can still be used by a VIP for a quick and clandestine getaway.

Platform 61 came to be by happenstance due to the Waldorf-Astoria being built in 1931 on the site of a former powerhouse used by Grand Central Terminal. The powerhouse had its own train platform for getting machinery and workman back and forth to the Terminal. With the powerhouse gone, the hotel planned on using the intact platform to transport well-heeled guests on special railcars, dropping them off at the platform. From there it was a short elevator ride straight into the hotel's lobby. This white glove service never quite panned out, but with the Waldorf often hosting US presidents and other dignitaries the platform began serving another purpose.

Often it would be readied in case a particular VIP needed to come quietly in and out of the hotel for privacy or security sake. On record, the platform has only been officially used by one president—Franklin Delano Roosevelt. Unbeknownst to most of the public at the time, the president suffered from the effects of polio resulting in his inability to walk. The secret service used platform 61 to hide his affliction from the public. Agents would carry the president by chair to a nondescript door that led to the hotel's garage. He was placed in his Pierce-Arrow limousine which was driven into a freight elevator just outside the hotel's garage on 49th Street. (Luckily the body of the limousine was narrow enough to fit into the just 6-foot-wide elevator.) When the elevator reached the train platform it simply drove into the waiting private freight car. It's unknown how many times he used the secret platform, but secret service logs confirm at least once in 1944, when Roosevelt took the presidential train from New York City to his private residence in New Hyde Park, New York.

Incredibly the freight railcar that Roosevelt used is still parked on nearby Track 63. Though it has never been absolutely confirmed as part of Roosevelt's presidential train, it has all the tell tale signs. The railcar has armored siding, bullet resistant glass, and gun turrets. Another sign—the extra suspension said to give the train more stabilization and thus a smoother ride for the disabled president. The railcar is stuck for the time being, if not forever, because its armored sides prove to be too heavy for it

to be moved out of the area today.

Other dignitaries known to use the platform were Generals John J. Pershing and Douglas MacArthur and Illinois Governor Adlai Stevenson.

Over the decades the area around Platform 61 was used in some rather eclectic ways. In 1948, Filene's Department Store put on a fashion show here and in 1965, pop artist Andy Warhol hosted an "underground" party on the platform.

At one point the railcar was being used by the Waldorf to store kitchen items and in the 1970s and 1980s homeless people used the area as a place to get out of the elements.

Nowadays security is much higher for a number of reasons. For one, though the MTA will not positively confirm it, word is a diesel train is often stationed idling at the platform, just in case the president needs to be spirited off Manhattan Island in case of an emergency.

Former MTA head Peter Kalikow learned this first hand in 2003. According to the book, *Grand Central—How a Train Station Transformed America*, by Sam Roberts, Mr. Kalikow was nearby the platform inspecting the East Side Access Construction project when he offered to take his guests to look at the Roosevelt train car.

Suddenly out of the darkness a secret service officer confronted the group. One

of Kalikow's aides gestured to him and said, "It was his train station." The agent politely responded, "Not today." Later the group found out then President George W. Bush was in town meeting with the United Nations General Assembly and the area was secured for a potential escape route.

Though special tours are sometimes permitted you may get a chance to see it for yourself—passengers on outbound Metro-North trains often catch a glimpse of it if they are traveling on one of the more eastern outbound track.

INFO BOOTH

The information booth with its iconic brass clock on top in the center of Grand Central Terminal is likely the most recognizable place in the terminal, if not the city. Since the building has been open, "Meet me at the clock at Grand Central" has been an utterance millions have made for countless rendezvous.

And of course the booth is important for its original intent too: giving out information. The MTA says the booth's attendants field over one thousand questions every hour. As for the clock on top, one might want to set their watch to it. As well as all the others clocks in the terminal, is set by the atomic clock at the Naval Observatory in Bethesda, Maryland. Their timekeeping is said to be accurate to within one second every 1.4 million years.

Close observers may notice the information booth has no doors on the outside. Rather there is a hidden circular staircase in the center cylinder of the booth which takes employees to the floor below.

FEDERAL RESERVE BANK GOLD VAULT

The Federal Reserve Bank of New York sits on winding Liberty Street in the heart of the Financial District. The building is oddly picturesque yet imposing. A literal fortress, its large bricked sides and heavily ironed barred windows conjure up feelings of strength and reliance. Justly so, for the amount of wealth inside is absolutely staggering: some half million gold bars are stored here. "The Fed" as it is know is one of the most secure places in the world. However, would you believe, with a bit of work and planning, little ole' you, can actually see it for yourself. No, not behind eight inches of bullet proof glass or on some remote monitor, but deep, down in one of the lowest points of Manhattan.

The Federal Reserve Bank of New York is one of twelve banks in the United States Federal Reserve System which help regulate the country's financial institutions and keep the economy healthy. Often referred to as the "the nation's piggy bank," the Federal Reserve also puts money in and out of circulation, destroying paper bills deemed too old or worn.

But the New York Federal Reserve Bank's more "colorful" purpose is the gold vault—the only Federal Reserve bank to have one and also the world's largest. Over

6,000 tons is stored here, almost a quarter of the world's supply.

These gold owners include central banks, foreign governments and official international organizations. None of it is owned by private hands or entities, nor by the Federal Reserve System. The "Fed" merely acts as a guardian and custodian of the gold with a lot of it first coming here around World War II. During that time of instability, other countries found this the safest place to store their gold reserves—much of whom used gold as the basis of their economies. Deposits peaked in 1973 when the US stopped converting dollars into gold for foreign governments. At one point 12,000 tons of gold was stored here. And the cost of all this security? There is no separate charge for gold storage but all of the countries and international organizations storing gold have accounts with the Federal Reserve and use other services as well. Why such a bargain? Because it is simply much more in the United States' best interest to provide a secure place for the world's gold rather than make a profit from the endeavor.

Despite being one of the most populated areas in the world, downtown New York City is actually a very smart place to store all this gold. First off, the Fed's vault is chiseled out of natural bedrock some eighty feet below ground level. It is one of the deepest rooms in all of Manhattan. Not only does the bedrock make it impenetrable but also capable of holding the incredible mass weight in gold.

And as said before, almost anyone can see the gold for themselves. Free tours are available, but are very limited. Be ready to book online weeks in advance and possibly have a background check done.

The tour is a wonderfully strange dichotomy. Upon entering the building, one is surrounded by intimidating state of the art security and well-armed officers. One can feel eyes on them at all times. But there is also an air of cordiality and openness. Tour guides cheerfully escort the group first through the teller building pointing out interesting exhibits like the teller stations complete with their ornate bars and vaulted Rafael Guastavino-tiled ceilings, all the while explaining the history of the Fed until it is time to reach the grand finale: The gold vault.

After a non-eventful elevator ride below, the doors open up to the incredible vault entrance which consists of a ninety-ton cylinder with an walkway through the center. This is the only opening into the vault. To secure the entrance, the nine-foot-high cylinder is turned, closing off the walkway, and four very large steel rods secure it into place. Time clocks lock the cylinder creating an impassable barrier. The seal is so tight,

once the cylinder is closed only about seventy hours of oxygen remains to sustain one person.

The vault's interior looks strangely similar to a very clean locker room. Row after row of brightly painted aqua blue steel lockers hold the gold. Not that the gold could be missed. Its brilliance and the amount seems unreal. The mostly uniform gold bricks look almost fake, like cheap movie props, seemingly too glittery to be actual gold.

Each bar has stamped coded numbers and symbols detailing origin, date of cast,

ownership and purity. None of the gold is 100% pure. Additives like silver, platinum, cooper, and iron have to be put in the bars or they will not hold their shape.

Numbers are assigned to all the lockers so as to not reveal the ownership of the gold. All of them are also padlocked and have two additional combination locks. Whenever any locker is opened, two gold vault staff members and a federal reserve staff auditor must be present.

In the middle of vault is the giant scale for measuring the gold. Deposits and

withdrawals are weighed on this scale as needed. Almost looking cartoonish in size, it's actually a very specialized piece of equipment. When gold is weighed the ventilation system must be turned off because the scale is so sensitive. Gold handlers must wear magnesium foot protectors because each bar weighs around a hefty 27 and half pounds.

After all that ooh and ahhing of the gold it is time to go back upstairs and thus back to reality. But the letdown is tempered thanks

to a parting gift from the Federal Reserve—a keepsake bag of shredded money put out of circulation.

DESTRUCTION OF MONEY

The Federal Reserve Bank system handles billions of dollars of paper currency everyday and one of the responsibilities of the Federal Reserve Bank of New York is to take worn money out of circulation. This is done at the East Rutherford Operations Center in New Jersey. Around five million dollars in paper currency is taken out of circulation every weekday.

The process starts when currency is deposited into the Operations Center where it is verified for deposit. During this process the money is put into a hi-tech machine which senses if each paper bill is still fit for circulation. The machine can process some 74,000 bills an hour. (This includes detecting counterfeits which are then inspected by hand for further investigation and forwarding to the US Secret Service.)

After the bills are deemed unfit they are taken out of circulation and replaced by new bills. The rejected bills are then fed into a shedder which cuts them into confetti-like pieces. About 26 percent of all the bills replaced are $1 bills which usually have a circulation expectancy of about 5.9 years. A $100 bill however can last up to around seven years.

FRIARS CLUB

The Friars Club is world famous for its celebrity roasts of honorees willing to be pelted with bawdy jokes at their expense. But the Friars is much more than a place to get zinged. For members, the club offers a fraternal atmosphere in the confines of its regal and historic clubhouse. It is a place for people in the entertainment business and beyond to talk shop, meet with peers, create and maintain long-lasting friendships.

The Friars membership roster past and present is nothing short of incredible in terms of showbiz royalty and dignitaries. For instance, Milton Berle, Frank Sinatra, Billy Crystal, Frank Sinatra, Jack Dempsey, W. C. Fields, Edward R. Murrow, Jimmy Kimmel, and Ronald Reagan just to name a very few have all been members.

But the Friars is not just for people in the arts and in fact twenty-five percent are in non-entertainment professions. Application to become a member usually starts with a recommendation from another member.

For those of the celebrity persuasion, the Friars is a bit of a safe haven. As club historian Barry Dougherty says, "For some of our known people it is also a place to not be harassed by fans and to be left in peace. They can entertain friends without being bothered."

Started in 1904, The Friars came about almost accidentally. At the time press agents were being taken advantage of when it came to their disbursement of free passes to live

entertainment shows. Passes were given to journalists as a way to garner positive publicity for the shows the agents represented. Apparently many of the passes were being sold on the secondary market. So the agents began meeting at Browne's Chop House to figure out a fix. They eventually found one, but also realized they enjoyed each other's companionship at the restaurant. Therefore they decided to form a club and the Friars Club was born. The name Friars was chosen because it derives from the Latin, frater, meaning "brother," which exemplified the spirit of the club. Their motto, *Prae Omnia Fraternitas*, means "all things brotherhood."

They built their first clubhouse, located on West 48th Street, in 1916, but unfortunately lost the building in 1933. After several locations that included rooms at the Edison Hotel, they moved into their current home at 57 East 55th Street in 1957. It is playfully known as "The Monastery." The place has the feel of an old English manor, perfect for a private New York City club. Sumptuous decor like carved oak wood paneling, deep hued marble pair nicely with the event rooms and social areas. Walls are lined with photographs, caricatures and mementos of past and current members. Rooms include the Billy Crystal Bar and the Frank Sinatra Dining Room where many events are held. Members can also enjoy the billiards room, fitness center and even an in-house barbershop and shoeshine.

Over the years, a club like this has of course chalked up numerous wonderful stories about its members. For instance Jackie Gleason used the pool table to practice daily for his role as Minnesota Fats in movie the *The Hustler*.

And known to almost anyone who has ever heard of The Friars Club, is their long tradition of putting on their celebrity roasts. The roasts consist of the "honoree" being the subject of humorous barbs, many of which would make many a man blush. The roasts began in 1950 and became popular with the public when they were televised off and on starting in the late sixties.

Fun and games aside, The Friars also has a charitable side and contributes to several public service causes every year and hold an annual Christmas and Chanukah party for underprivileged children with some 1,500 in attendance who receive toys and gifts.

FRICK BOWLING ALLEY

The Frick Collection on 5th and East 70th Street is one of the most impressive private art museums in New York, if not the world. Named after industrialist Henry Clay Frick whose personal art collection was the nucleus of this collection, the museum was built first as his family's personal residence then after his death became a museum.

Not only did he amass one of the greatest art collections in the world, his former home is the epitome of the Gilded Age. Built in 1914, it is a monumental work of art with hand cut marble, among the flourishes. With its open center garden court and seemingly endless cavernous rooms, some with grandiose themes, it is easy to forget this was once a home.

Though all this opulence and beauty continues to impress visitors today, some would be equally impressed, perhaps even shocked, to know the place also features a bowling alley.

Yes, with all its priceless works of art, austere decor and manicured grounds, the basement has a bowling alley. As one would expect this is not one's neighborhood bowling alley where a couple of guys come in to sling some balls and drink beers. Along with the rest of the home, the alley and subsequent recreation room is exquisitely executed and designed as one would hope when a gilded-ager gets their hands on a popular sport.

Tightly fitted into a small space, the two lane alley made by the Brunswicke-Balke-Collender Company features ornate vaulted plaster ceilings, and carved mahogany-paneled walls. There's also a billiard room nearby done in equally careful execution and luxury.

Like many bowling alleys, the lanes are constructed of maple and pine, and for its era do not feature set up machines for the pins. Instead servants stood by and put the pins up by hand.

The original bowling balls are still here, made of a Bakelite composite common for the time, and with only two holes, not three for the bowlers' fingers.

The ball return is especially unique with its carved flourishes and ornate posts. Again no automation here, just good old fashioned gravity and physics to return the balls. A chalkboard off to the side was used for keeping score.

Frick himself was a stickler when it came to recording household costs. Luckily for the museum curators, for they have all the receipts for building and maintaining the bowling alley. The alley cost a princely $850 dollars to build with the balls costing an extra $100.

Henry Frick died in 1919—only giving him a few years to reside here. After his death, his daughter Helen Clay Frick took over the home and created what was first called the Frick Art Reference Library. Her life's work was amassing numerous books and documents for the museum from the United States and Europe. As the collection grew she began running out of space to store the items and the bowling alley became storage for the collection.

That very well may have saved the alley's originality before it was restored in 1997, the space had remained virtually untouched, inadvertantly sealed from the changes of time. It is pretty much the status of the bowling alley today. Frick administrators say due to the fragility of the interior and lack of fire exits, they cannot open it to the general public. There is however a workaround. According to their website, donate $5,000 as a "Supporting Fellow Level" and you'll get the privilege of seeing the alley up close and personal. Mister Frick would probably crack a smile about that.

HENRY CLAY FRICK

Though his taste in art was exquisite, Henry Clay Frick was not the necessarily the most well-liked person. In fact, Frick had the dubious honor of being once labeled "America's most hated man" partly due to his anti-union actions.

Courtesy of The Frick Collection

Frick made his fortune in steel and coal. When he partnered with fellow financier Andrew Carnegie, together they built the Carnegie Steel Company into one of the largest steel companies in the world. Frick would go onto help build the United States Steel Company.

But Frick's reputation will always have a blot due to the infamous Homestead, Pennsylvania Strike in 1892. The Carnegie Steel Company was in a bitter labor dispute with its workers. The strike came to a violent head, when Frick hired 300 strikebreakers—armed agents from the Pinkerton Detective agency—to essentially invade the mill. An all out battle ensued leaving ten killed and sixty wounded. The country was outraged calling it a massacre and vilifying Frick. An anarchist even tried to assassinate him, shooting Frick twice and stabbing him multiple times. Incredibly, Frick managed to be back at work in a week.

The Homestead Strike followed Frick for the rest of his life and contributed to the downfall of his friendship with Carnegie. Years later, when Carnegie was near death, he requested to meet with Frick to which Frick responded in note, "Tell him I'll see him in Hell."

Actually known as quiet and reserved, Frick was perhaps not as purely ruthless as he is often depicted. When he died in 1919, he left a staggering fifty-million dollar fortune. Five-sixths of it was donated to charity.

GARMENT DISTRICT EATERIES

Lunch in a loading dock or hallway? Many would scoff at the idea, perhaps even be a little repulsed. But for many workers in New York City's Garment District, these little eateries are not only a necessity, but actually quite tasty, and for some, provide a little taste of home.

Much more insider than any downtown bistro, these lunch counters are tucked into the Garment District building's loading docks and side entrances—often only known by local workers. Sometimes called "freight entrance restaurants" they are part entrepreneurship, ingenuity, and a bit of stubbornness. The places are set up as an alternative to the more expensive and crowded eateries around the neighborhood and offer up a cheaper and more home-cooked alternative.

Often just a tiny sign or a line snaking outside the side of a building is the only indication of where a lunch counter has set up shop. Most are bare bones, stripped down lunch counters, serving up inexpensive, but quality ethnic food. Due to sky-high rents in the area, the owners of these places have had to resort in creative and unconventional ways of renting space. These eateries can be found in hallways, loading docks, entranceways or anywhere they can put a stove, some counters, and a refrigerator. Thanks to the diversity of garment district workers, the lunch counters offer a diverse selection of food. There is kosher, Chinese, Spanish, and more. The food is good, if not excellent. Want proof? Count how many delivery people are standing in line. Besides, if a restaurant is located in a loading dock, it has got be doing something right. These

are not fly by night places; they all registered with the health department and most have an "A" rating.

This odd pairing of industrial space with the culinary arts makes for interesting bedfellows. Walking into rather drab loading docks with the scents from the simmering stoves is quite the juxtaposition. Delivery men with large, squeaky-wheeled racks of clothing carefully and politely maneuver pass people ordering their lunch. It is a delivery entrance after all. The eateries' owners greet their customers with familiarity, no doubt they are regulars. The lunchtime lines show quite a diverse cross-section of garment district workers, including textile workers, delivery men, and fashionistas.

Some take it to go in styrofoam containers overloaded with the special of the day, others sit at the short counters—no doubt their only quiet time for the day.

Among the eating establishments is Nick's Place, which calls itself the "Best kept secret in the Garment District." Its previous owner was from Poland so there is a Eastern Europe influence here. Pork pirogi or cabbage, mushroom, and onion-filled pirogi on Fridays. But there are standards like burgers and Greek diner standbys like pitas and stuffed grape leaves. Nick's Place has even ingeniously added enough tables to offer table service in their tiny corner of the world.

On West 37th Street there is El Sabroso and Arie's Cafe both serving Spanish food. El Sabroso, an Ecuadorean restaurant has

been in business for over twenty years. Owner Tony Molina oversees his stove and checks in on his patrons as he prepares chicken, and roast pork, roast chicken, roast lamb himself just mere feet away from the customers. An order includes all for well under $10.

At Arie's Cafe, Dominican food is the specialty. Once a garment factory worker himself, owner Rodolfo Pérez opened in a space so tight he uses his waist high refrigerator as a counter—opening and closing it dozens of times a day. He says all this maneuvering and workarounds to open a lunch counter in a place like this is worth it, "Look at the people. They work hard and I want to take care of them. It's not always all about money. I like to make people happy."

THE GARMENT DISTRICT

Though less than a square mile in size, The garment district has been known since the early 20th century as the world's epicenter of fashion design and manufacturing. Nowhere else is there more of a concentration of fashion businesses. Every aspect from design to selling is done here and includes businesses like showrooms, fashion labels, manufacturers and supplies. The district is generally considered to be between Fifth and Ninth avenues and between 34th and 42nd streets.

New York City became the garment leader of the United States first in part because of slavery. Southern owners found it more economical to have Northern manufacturers make clothing for slaves rather than themselves. The US Civil War further increased demand for New York City's garment services with steady need for manufactured uniforms.

As Americans began to have more of their clothing manufactured rather than made by themselves, the garment manufacturers in New York City began to congregate for convenience and low rent in what was then the red light district of Midtown Manhattan known as the "Tenderloin District." Immigrants were pushed into the area politically and economically, but were also often the very people working in the garment industry.

GOTHAM GREENS

It is one of last things New Yorkers would ever possibly think they could have readily available. Locally grown produce that is sometimes even sold just steps from where it was grown and available year round.

Gotham Greens is the reason for this little miracle. They are a local produce company using state of the art greenhouses and hydroponics technology for growing vegetables on something New York City has plenty of: rooftops.

The company has locations in Greenpoint and Gowanus, Brooklyn as well as in Hollis, Queens. Along with a facility in Chicago, Illinois, they are the largest urban agriculture company in the world. Started in 2009 by Viraj Puri and Eric Haley, Gotham Greens grows over a dozen kinds of vegetables; mostly leafy greens including kale, basil, bok choy and assorted lettuce like butterhead and a leafy version of iceberg. Baby tomatoes and herbs are also grown on a smaller scale.

Their produce can be found all over: from gourmet and specialty shops to chain supermarkets local restaurants. Buyers include local chefs who use the ultra-fresh produce in their upscale restaurants and special catering events. Ironically some of Gotham's produce eventually does indeed travel a long distance—Delta Airlines serves some of their greens during select flights.

Leafy greens is their chief crop, almost a no-brainer in this crazy-for-salad city. Also because greens and are highly perishable and usually shipped from long distances like California and Mexico, locally grown makes perfect sense. And lest us forget the lowered fuel consumption in shipping.

Almost unheard of a few years ago, Gotham Greens has produce often picked in the morning and is on a lunch or dinner table that day. And it does not take a nutritionist to know produce picked just hours instead of days before is worlds apart. Leafy greens have a crunchier and fuller texture, are tastier, and have more nutrients intact. The company's Gowanus greenhouse is 20,000 square feet and is located rather symbolically enough on the roof of a Whole Foods Supermarket. (And yes, they do sell Gotham Greens.)

Gotham Greens grows over 20 million heads of lettuce yearly. The view from their rooftop greenhouses are quite striking. Miniature fields of varying greenery are neatly situated in their hydroponic pods. At their Greenpoint and Gowanus locations, one can see views of the Brooklyn and Manhattan skylines. The scents are overwhelming as one walks along the aisles of chest high plants enveloping one in fresh smells.

"Our plants are really coddled and looked after," says Nicole Baum, marketing manager at Gotham Greens. In addition to computers monitoring the greenhouse temperature, humidity, and carbon dioxide, growers are required to wear hairnets, aprons, and gloves when touching the plants. Also no GMOs are used in the growth of the plants.

Nicole says their custom hydroponic irrigation system is also a big part of the process. Gotham Greens recirculating water system uses ten times less water than conventional agriculture while eliminating all agricultural runoff. The company also tailors the nutritional recipes for each variety of greens. The result is a more nutritious, flavorful product.

Even the electricity is 100% renewable with windmills and solar panels encompassing the building generating energy. The overall greenhouse temperature can also be controlled using sensors that turn equipment like shade curtains, misting systems and windows off and on keeping the greenhouses a balmy 77°F year-round. An added benefit of the rooftop location is heat emanating from the building which helps keeps the plants warm during the winter.

In all, the company says it grows 20 to 30 times more produce per square yard than ground farming. But with all of this high-tech equipment and the fact the greenhouses are located in the city, they still have to deal with one of the biggest hardships in farming: pests. But instead of pesticide they use what they call "integrated pest management." It includes adhesive curtains to trap the insects and the introduction of other insects like praying mantis and ladybugs to feed on the detrimental pests.

Though this kind of farming seems pretty rosy, Gotham Greens is the first to say it is not the end all be all way for the future. Conventional farming is here to stay. They like to say they are not the only solution, not the best solution, just another solution. Though the greenhouse is off-limits because of food safety restrictions, the public can get a little peek of the greenhouses from their observation deck where they host weekly tours April through November—understandable considering these little beauties need to rest and grow.

GOWANUS CANAL

It is not hard to see the irony of Gotham Greens being located literally just feet away from one of the most contaminated waterways in the United States. The Gowanus Canal is often thought of synonymously with urban blight and unchecked industrialization.

Just under two miles long, the former creek is fed from the New York Bay which helped make it become a major industrial throughway since the early 1800s. Local manufacturers often used it as a dumping ground for their unwanted byproducts, chemicals, and raw sewage.

The Environmental Protection Agency has declared the canal a superfund site committing the federal government to invest in its longterm cleanup. Cost is expected to be at least a half a billion dollars.

Cleanup has begun, and there has been some signs of life reemerging. Every so often an animal like a beaver will be spotted in the canal, though hopefully, for the animal's sake, it's just a temporary visit. But even more unimaginable to many who have not only seen, but smelled the canal, there are some who actually enjoy canoeing and kayaking on the polluted waters.

GRAMERCY PARK

Gramercy Park has intrigued passing pedestrians daily since the 19th Century. Located between East 20th and 21st Street, its wrought iron fence seems to protect the genteel park from the modern world, leaving it to flourish with its abundance of greenery.

The park is two acres in size—a seemingly huge plot of open space by New York City's standards. It is meticulously maintained to the point of looking like a grand manor's garden. Founder and president of the Gramercy Park Block Association Arlene Harrison, who is also a Park Trustee says, "Samuel B. Ruggles created Gramercy Park pursuant to an 1831 indenture as a private ornamental park for the use, benefit, and enjoyment of the owners and occupants of the surrounding lots. It really should have been called 'Gramercy Garden' and not park, which is misleading." It is off-limits to the public, a private park in the middle of Manhattan. Some are disappointed, perhaps even miffed about this being so. But the story of Gramercy Park is really not one of exclusivity, but more of good neighborliness.

The name Gramercy is a corrupted form of the Dutch word *Crommesshie* meaning "crooked little swamp." It's hard to imagine but the park was indeed once a swamp. It was part of a farm owned by the James Duane, the first New York City Mayor.

Samuel B. Ruggles was a lawyer and politician who dabbled in land development and a proponent of open city spaces, so he bought the land in 1831. After putting quite a bit of money and effort draining the swamp and landscaping the land into a park in 1844, he then gated and locked it up to protect the plantings inside. His plan was to create a space for the exclusive use of the occupants of the buildings surrounding the park.

Essentially they would own a piece of the park and pay an annual fee for the upkeep.

Special gate keys made of gold were given out to residents. Over the decades they have included inventor Thomas Edison, author John Steinbeck, and actress Julia Roberts. Both Presidents Theodore Roosevelt and John F. Kennedy played in the park as children.

Though the gold keys have been replaced by rather bland and hard-to-copy Medeco-brand keys, but the rules of the park have changed little over the decades.

There are thirty-nine lot owner buildings with frontage on the park, and they have between one and four lots. Buildings pay a annual assessment of $8,000 per lot and receive 2 building keys per lot. Today 236 personal numbered keys have been purchased by residents living in thirty-nine lot owner buildings. Locks are changed yearly and losing one could cost a resident $1,000 to replace. Only five guests per key holder are allowed in at a time. And one might want to think twice before trying to sneak into the park without a key because one is required to get out too! Park rules include no alcohol, no smoking, dogs, bicycles, or recreation with balls or frisbees. Also feeding the squirrels and birds is a no-no.

A few of the lot owner institutions on the park are allowed to give guests access on a regular basis. Members of the The Players and the National Arts Club which surround the park are allowed access, as are members of the Brotherhood Synagogue, Calvary-St. George's Church, and the luxury Gramercy Park Hotel. However, hotel staff must personally escort them in and out of the the park.

Inside, visitors are greeted by winding pathways which are surrounded by well-manicured rounded boxwood plants. Little groups of various plantings dot the park. There is also a rather imposing elm tree, somewhat twisted and marked by time. It is the only original tree left in the park.

Ms. Harrison describes the daily routine of regular visitors to the park. In the early mornings come the walkers out to get a little exercise. Mid-morning the babies and young children along with their nannies or mothers come out. By the afternoon, children will visit after a day at school. By evening families are there to finish out the day. Weekends seem to be reserved for working people wanting a little peace and quiet, often to read. "You have to remember, this place is essentially these people's front yard," she says.

Over the years. the park has been open for special occasions. After the Draft Riots in 1863, Union Soldiers were allowed to use the park as a thank you for protecting the neighborhood from rioters. And for some

years the park was opened to the public one day every spring, but that no longer takes place. Still, if one really wants to experience Gramercy Park for themselves Christmas Eve is their ticket. The park is open that evening to the public every year.

Along with the manicured grounds, at one end of the park is an Alexander Calder sculpture entitled, "Janey Waney" on loan from the Calder Foundation. And sitting prominently in the center of the park is an imposing bronze statue of 19th century Shakespearean actor Edwin Booth who

lived nearby at The Players. Booth is also known as the brother of John Wilkes Booth who assassinated Abraham Lincoln. The statue depicts Booth in the Shakespearean play *Hamlet*. It was given to the park by "The Players" as a gift in 1913.

Again, the exclusivity of the park can rub some the wrong way. Some cry elitism, however they fail to understand the park land is indeed privately owned and maintained with private funds. It is no different than someone's private front yard. The owners contend the park is closed off to protect the delicate plantings and original historic artifacts inside. It is understandable when inside for there is a different feel to this park than others in New York City. There is tranquility and order here. Not a speck of trash can be found. The park is serenely quiet as if visitors understand the shared solitude afforded by one another.

BOOTH AND HIS BROTHER

Perhaps one of the most extraordinary and ironic stories in American history involved actor Edwin Booth.

Somewhere around 1863 and 1865, he was on a crowded train platform in Jersey City, waiting to buy tickets. Suddenly a teenaged male noticed a man lose his footing and begin slipping between a slow-moving train and the gap between it and the platform. Booth grabbed him in the nick of time avoiding serious injury or possibly death.

Less than a year later Booth's brother would kill the young man's father—Abraham Lincoln.

When Robert Lincoln was saved by Booth, He knew full well who the famous actor was even calling him out by name to thank him and often recalled the story. Booth had no idea until later when receiving letters from General Ulysses S. Grant and Colonel Adam Badeau who happened to be a friend of Booth's.

Robert Lincoln at the time was serving as an officer under the staff of Grant and relayed the story to both men. Booth was told told if there was anything the U. S. Government could do for him to ask. After his brother murdered the president, Edwin actually did try to call in the favor, requesting his brother's body to be released to his family but was turned down.

Edwin was always haunted by his brother's actions yet was said to take some solace in the fact that he saved the president's son's life.

GRAND CENTRAL M-42

Over 750,000 people visit Grand Central Terminal every day, but few know they are walking over a little-known basement so secret it does not even appear on Grand Central's blueprints. It was only in the 1980s that station officials even confirmed it existed. Known simply as "M-42," it was a place Adolf Hitler was even rumored to have wanted to sabotage during World War II. So important was this area, soldiers were stationed there with a shoot-to-kill order if anyone unauthorized tried to enter. And even today its exact location is still concealed.

So why all the cloak and dagger? M-42 is basically where electricity is converted from DC to AC to power all the trains. At three hundred feet below, M-42 is one of the deepest rooms in all of Manhattan and is actually dug out of bedrock which also makes it one of the most secure spots in the city. (Today one can actually see the bedrock which was dug out to create M-42. Much of it was dumped for use as rail beds along the Metro-North rail line along the Hudson River.)

Ironically to enter M-42, one begins by going through a nondescript door in one of the busiest sections of the terminal. From there it is thirteen stories down a series of staircases which are literally carved and blasted out of the bedrock. (One can actually still see the chisel and blast marks.)

During World War II these rotary converters were deathly important for supplying electricity to the train system on the Eastern Seaboard. Eighty percent of all troop and supply movements to ships from New York to Europe were along these tracks, not to mention the regular usage by ordinary American citizens.

Destroying the converters would put an unimaginable burden on the American war effort. What is almost unfathomable, was how easy it could be to destroy the converters. The machinery was so sensitive, simply throwing a bucket of sand onto the exposed spinning copper components would destroy them immediately. Therefore during the war, M-42 was heavily guarded with troops ordered to shoot on sight if a saboteur came down the staircase with a bucket of sand.

A group of German saboteurs actually did managed to get into Grand Central Terminal. According to Sam Roberts, author of *Grand Central: How a Train Station Transformed America,* the men managed to come ashore from U-boats on the coast of Amagansett, Long Island in 1942. They apparently rendezvoused at the information booth, but there is no positive confirmation the saboteurs were here to destroy the rotary converters and were soon arrested before they could do any damage.

Once below, the doorway opens to a cavernous space full of modern electrical equipment all humming and buzzing away. But by far the most interesting site are the three giant antique rotary converters once used to convert AC to DC power for the trains. Long out of commission, these machines have earned their right to spend retirement here. For these are the very items Hitler was said to be wanting to search out and destroy.

ANTIQUE COMPUTER

The converters are not the only fascinating piece of history down in M-42. Nearby, the rotary converters are in a row of what looks to be a telephone switchboard system. The equipment is actually one of the earliest electric computers still in existence, dating from all the back to 1912. Now long since retired, the system was used to determine locations of trains when they stalled in the tunnels. Cords were strung along the rail lines and if the train stalled, a cord pulled by a conductor which rang a bell on the computer. It would then compute where the cord was pulled and print its location on a ticker tape.

By 1922 radio communication became the standard and this system was scraped but kept here for posterity.

HALL OF GREAT AMERICANS

There is seemingly a "Hall of Fame" for everything these days. Of course there is the Baseball Hall of Fame and the Rock and Roll Hall of Fame, and then there are Hall of Fames for cowboys, firemen, and not to mention for dozens of other occupations. And lest one forget, practically every organized sport has one. Even the Barbie doll has her own Hall of Fame.

But few have ever heard of the first American Hall of Fame. The one that begat all the others. The Hall of Fame for Great Americans is now all but forgotten, but decades ago it was the high watermark in honoring the achievements of individual American citizens. Its recipients were as highly regarded as Nobel Peace prize winners. Newspaper columnists and ordinary folks argued passionately about worthy nominees. There were also concerted and organized efforts made by groups and organizations to get their favorites into it.

It was so much in the American consciousness, even the movie *Wizard of Oz* referenced it, "You will be a bust, be a bust, be a bust in the Hall of Fame!" sing the Munchkins to Dorothy.

The Hall of Fame for Great Americans actually even has a physical location which is situated on the campus of Bronx Community College in University Heights. There behind the campus' main library is a stately 630-foot open-aired arched colonnade. Its location is appropriate for such an honor for it is the highest natural point in The Bronx

NEW·YORK·VNIVERSITY·CHARTERED·MDCCCXXXI
VNIVERSITY·HEIGHTS·PVRCHASED·MDCCCXCI
VNIVERSITY·COLLEGE·REMOVED·MDCCCXCIV
THIS·HALL·OF·FAME·WAS·COMPLETED·MCM
IN·HONOR·OF·GREAT·AMERICANS

and one of the highest in the entire city. Perhaps even more symbolically, it is also the area where the British Army camped during occupation then were subsequently run out by then General George Washington in 1776.

Along the Hall of Fame's colonnade are bronze busts bearing the likenesses of 98 Hall of Fame members including notable statesmen, artists, inventors, philanthropists and explorers. The busts are nothing to sniff at, made by some of the finest sculptors of their times. Each bust was specifically created for the honor and was not allowed to be copied for 50 years after completion. Below each bust is a bronze tablet with the member's name, a commemoration, achievements, and quotations.

The Hall of Fame was the brainchild of then New York University Chancellor Henry Mitchell MacCracken, which at the time was the campus' location. McCracken said he was inspired by Germany's Hall of Fame, The Ruhmeshalle in Munich, feeling the United States and its citizens were worthy of a similar place of honor.

This was a time when the United States was still overcoming a bit of an inferiority complex with Europe. Though it was quickly becoming a leader of the world, and the nation often roiled itself in European-esque trappings. Many buildings of great stature like universities and courthouses of this time were built to look like their European and Roman counterparts. Therefore, it was only appropriate for the United States to create a Hall of Fame to celebrate the extraordinary Americans generated from this great land of liberty.

The limestone and brick colonnade was completed in 1900 and was formally dedicated on May 30, 1901. The design by famed architect Stanford White, who also built some of the neighboring buildings, is similar in its Beaux Arts design.

As for Hall of Fame members, many are right out of the pages of American history books including George Washington, Harriet Breecher Stowe, and Thomas Edison. Others seem fairly obscure to 21st century minds. (Charlotte Cushman, Mark Hopkins, Rufus Choate, anyone?)

Requirements were short to be eligible for the Hall of Fame. A person had to be a born here or a naturalized citizen, contributed to America's economic, political, or cultural endeavors, and have had been dead for at least ten years (then after 1922, 25 years deceased). A simple majority vote ensured one's membership into the Hall. The board of electors were no slouches either, made up of notables like Helen Keller, Grover Cleveland, and physicist Robert Oppenheimer.

The country embraced the Hall of Fame immediately. Organizations like the

American Bar Association would get behind a nominee. Fevered editorials ran in newspapers expounding or denigrating the nominees. The induction ceremonies were equally revered, attended by enthusiastic crowds. Future Hall of Famer Thomas Edison was on hand to unveil the bust of scientist Joseph Henry at a ceremony in 1924.

Through the decades, interest in the Hall of Fame waned; a casualty of lack of funding, changing tastes and competition from other hall of fames.

In 1973, budget constraints forced NYU to sell its Bronx Campus which in a way sealed the fate of the Hall. The final election was held in 1976. Four inductees still have no bust.

Today the Hall of Fame sits quietly, somewhat forgotten. Thousands visited it in its heyday, making it a must-do stop. The school does its part keeping the Hall tidy and over the years restorations have gone on. For the most part, the colonnade is a passageway for many students just to get from one class to another.

GOULD LIBRARY

Stanford White's Hall of Great Americans visually buttresses what is considered the architect's great masterpiece—the Gould Memorial Library. Built in 1900 he took inspiration from The Pantheon in Rome for this beaux arts landmark. Even today many argue this is one of the most opulent and exquisitely designed interiors in all of New York City.

Inside is the Great Reading Room—a soaring rotunda surrounded by marble Corinthian columns with Greek muse statues lining the upper balcony. Tiffany-made stained-glass windows and Italian-style mosaic floor designs all add to the dramatic space. The massive bronze doors at the entrance ended up becoming a memorial to Stanford White after he was murdered in 1906. His son Lawrence designed them with friends as tribute to White. The rest of the building is no longer used as a library by the college, but is often used as an assembly and event space.

HALLETT SANCTUARY

With over forty-two million people visiting Central Park every year, there is not much of the place that has not been traipsed, trampled and walked through. However there is one spot in the park few have ever heard of, much less have visited. A place unique not only for its seclusion but also as a window into Manhattan Island before civilization showed up.

Hallett Sanctuary is a three and a half acre parcel of land situated near Central Park's Southeast edge, wrapping around what is known as "The Pond." Many pass by, but few see the sign and wooden gates marking this special place. Closed off from the public for decades, Hallett Sanctuary has been allowed to grow and evolve naturally for some time. Critters like rabbits, squirrels and even the occasional woodchuck can be seen scurrying about in what is essentially the middle of Manhattan. The result is a parcel of land that looks like Manhattan did before mankind arrived. Now slowly and very limitedly it is being opened to the public.

Winding wood chipped trails take visitors through areas filled with New York native plants and wildflowers like Dutchman's breeches, shooting stars and trillium, which are now rarely seen in any part of the city. Trees in the sanctuary have been left alone to grow to massive sizes, and those that have fallen are left to rot all in the name of helping the overall ecosystem of the sanctuary.

Also present are large rock formations of ancient Manhattan schist protruding out of the ground. Ironically, the same bedrock is used to anchor the very buildings that surround the park.

One of the more popular spots at Hallett is high atop the rocky promontory which stands above "The Pond." A trickling waterfall attracts a good amount of birds splashing about. However there is a small reminder that the park is still indeed in the city: the waterfall's source is a simple garden hose.

For many non-New Yorkers, Hallett Sanctuary is perhaps a bit of a letdown. On the surface, notwithstanding the massive chunks of schist, the area looks pretty much like many wooded areas across North America. But for New Yorkers used to carefully planned, manicured and maintained spaces, the sanctuary is striking. The lush greenery creates a wooded and leafy cocoon around casual strollers who can quickly forget they are actually surrounded by a great metropolis. Only the occasional honking horn, siren or high buildings seemingly peeking through the vegetation remind visitors where they actually are.

The Central Park Conservancy, a nonprofit private organization managing the park, has carefully and painstakingly worked for years restoring the Hallett Sanctuary to its original form. Its road to a true urban oasis has be a long and challenging one.

In 1857 the area was known as "The Promontory." Central Park designers Frederick Law Olmsted and Calvert Vaux purposely left this and the surrounding swamp undisturbed in hopes of creating a bird sanctuary. The plans never came to fruition, and the swamp was drained and replaced by "The Pond." In 1934 then NYC Parks commissioner Robert Moses, an avid bird watcher himself, declared the area a bird sanctuary, banishing most of the public. As with other parts of Central Park, the sanctuary became a popular stopover for migrating birds on the Atlantic Flyway route.

However the lack of care over the decades actually harmed the area due to the overgrowth of invasive plants like wisteria, Norway maples, ailanthus and Japanese knotgrasses. There was also the pesky problem of homeless people moving into the area.

In 1986, the Sanctuary was renamed after George Hervey Hallett Jr., executive secretary of the Citizens Union of the City of New York and another avid birdwatcher. In 2001 the Conservancy began to restore the area in earnest.

Great care and research was taken to make get the sanctuary back to its "natural" state, which not only included weeding and planting, but hauling out decades of human trash.

Visitors are now given limited access to the sanctuary so as to give plants time to grow back and birds time to nest. Visitors do not not seem to mind, sometimes waiting almost an hour to get into this tiny space. During migratory season, there is no public access.

All of this hard work bringing the spot back to its natural state seems to be working. In 2006, an adventurous coyote somehow made his way into Hallett Sanctuary. Appropriately nicknamed "Hal", he was eventually caught and taken to an animal rehabilitation center in Upstate New York.

STREET POSTS

A sort of right of passage for all New Yorkers is getting lost in the park. No, not "send in a search party" lost, just a temporary loss of bearings. Obviously, this is not the Grand Canyon; just keep walking one direction and eventually everyone will be back on a city street.

But there is another way to always know where you are in Central Park. Just look for the nearest park light post. On their bases are a series of numbers. With them, visitors can pinpoint where they are in the park and the closest exit to the street. For instance, the first few numbers reveal the closest cross street, and the last number being odd (west side) or even (east side) tells which side of town. For those who just say "Use your phone's GPS," don't spoil the fun for rest of us.

HOLLOW BROWNSTONES

On gently sloping Joralemon Street in Brooklyn Heights are rows of elegant and rather dignified 19th-century townhouses, part of one of the most picturesque and beloved neighborhoods in the city.

At number 58 even the casual passerby will notice something askew, perhaps even amiss, with this three story townhouse. Its completely blacked out windows set against its uniformly red painted bricks are the first obvious signs. The structure is too neat and orderly; there is no "lived-in" feel to it. No tossed toys littering the front or manicured flower beds in the short front yard, rather there are large ugly metal plates draping the curb.

A secret lair for a superhero? A mobster's hangout? No, most might be a little disappointed with its somewhat utilitarian purpose.

Though the Mass Transit Authority has no official comment, 58 Joralemon Street is said to house a ventilation system for the city's subway system. The equipment helps pump in and out fresh air into the 4 and 5 subway line running below. Still there is some intrigue to the place. One can catch a glimpse through the crack between the townhouse's front doors which seemingly lead to another set of rather forbidding and forlorn looking doors inside reading, "Electrical Distribution Room."

The Greek Revival structure was once actually a home, built in 1847. The Interborough Rapid Transit Company took it over in 1908 and gutted and hollowed it out for its current use.

Neighbors ofter refer to 58 Joralemon as the "Shaft House," saying they will occasionally spy a worker or two entering the building. Now and then they can also hear the

415
Bruckner Blvd.

blades of the ventilator whipping around in a low pitched hum.

Some online sleuths surmise 58 Joralemon is also a secret train exit/station for emergencies. There are some telltale signs of the building that back up this theory. For one, the fire hose pipe right inside the curb of 58 is labeled, "Joralemon Street Tunnel IRT 4,5 Line NYC Transit." On the door of the building is a steel door handle with faded magic marker scribblings stating "EXIT #1."

Ventilators are common in the city, providing air to tunnels and subways, but normally they take a more industrial grade look. To some, 58 Joralemon is "laughably fake," but it is also an ingenious fake, for the city's infrastructure sometimes dictates that big, ugly pieces of equipment be plopped into places where they are least desired. Yet city planners found this workaround all the way back in 1908.

KAUFFMANN ASTORIA STUDIOS

Just steps from the 7 Train in the Greek neighborhood of Astoria, Queens sits a slice of Hollywood—the Kaufman Astoria Studios. Believe it or not, it is the biggest studio east of California. It is a full production facility in which film companies lease their studio space and services to produce film and television shows.

You have undoubtably been entertained by something made here. Everything from Oscar winning films, television classics, game shows, music videos, commercials and even today's fast growing internet series.

Names read like a history of American entertainment going back all the way to silent films and some of the first talkies. Like, The Marx Brothers first two films, *The Cocoanuts* and *Animal Crackers* as well as the first Sherlock Holmes movie in sound, *The Return of Sherlock Holmes* were filmed here. Classics like *Moonstruck, Scent of a Woman,* and some of Woody Allen's better known films including *Radio Days* also shot scenes here. The classic children's television series *Sesame Street* has taped at Kaufman Astoria for decades and, more recently, the Netflix series *Orange is the New Black*.

Kaufman Astoria consists of seven large stages including a massive one 26,000 square feet in size. Stages include everything from carpentry shops and audience seating, to hair, make-up and dressing rooms and production offices. The film sets look deceptively simple and rickety. From behind one can spy a hodgepodge of plywood, two-by-fours, and other materials. But remember, this is a visual medium, and it is all part of the illusion.

Kaufman Astoria Studio's home in Queens, New York makes sense considering the evolution and history of the film industry. Since their inception, movies have always been made in New York City and the surrounding area. In fact the world's first film studio was actually created by Thomas A. Edison in West Orange, New Jersey. During the early part of the 20th Century, several studios began to spring up in New Jersey and in New York City. Once film's popularity grew, there was a need for talent and filmmakers needed to look no further than Broadway to find ready and willing actors and actresses.

As the movie industry began to gravitate to the West Coast due to sunny weather and some say for tax reasons and other profit schemes, productions in Astoria began to wane. Beginning in World War II the US Army took control of the facility, using it to make propaganda and training films. Some of those who worked on them include director Frank Capra and actors Jimmy Stewart and John Wayne.

In 1976 it was designated a landmark on the National Register of Historic Places and a year later the Astoria Motion Pictures and Television Center Foundation was formed to preserve the facilities. In 1980, real estate

developer George S. Kaufman was given the opportunity to renovate and revive what is today known as Kaufman Astoria Studios.

Today Kaufmann Astoria Studios is in a halcyon era. Partly due to the tax breaks given to film productions in New York, the entire state has seen a boom in terms of film productions. This resurgence has led to the expansion of Kaufman Astoria which now includes the only backlot in New York City— 34,800 square foot outdoor space allows for filming outdoor scenes and scenes too big for indoor sets and without having to go on location. In fact, the backlot is so big it required the de-mapping of nearby 36th Street.

But with all these goings on, unfortunately the studio cannot be open to the public. Safety issues, privacy and even copyrights and intellectual property are just some of the reasons.

KNICKERBOCKER HOTEL DOOR

Most people riding the S subway train have seen it. Off to the side of the Times Square platform is a rather drab looking metal door. Most might think it is nothing more than a utility closet or maintenance room. But one's curiosity is stirred looking atop the doorway at a stone facade reading "KNICKERBOCKER HOTEL."

Though now locked for decades the door was once an effortless way for Knickerbocker Hotel patrons to head straight to the hotel's bar, lobby, and restaurant. When the hotel was built in 1906, this little entranceway led into a luxurious hall complete with fine furniture and decor. Once considered New York's most opulent hotel, the Knickerbocker was built by John Jacob Astor. The door was a rather savvy undertaking on his part. A section of the subway crossed over his property line. So he used this as leverage to have the Knickerbocker doorway built on the subway platform in 1901. It afforded patrons straight access to the hotel without them hitting the streets. Additionally, because there was no subway entrance on the very busy 42nd Street southwest side, the doorway persuaded many to go through the hotel to reach the station.

The hotel was recently been renovated to its original splendor, but the corridor behind the Knickerbocker door remains closed. It is mostly used for storage, but remnants of its glory days are still present. Faded original stenciling in an Art Nouveau motif can be seen here and there among the crumbling plaster. Though in disrepair, perhaps too much to be ever restored, the space gives a wonderful urban archeological peek into early 20th Century opulence.

MANHATTAN WELL MURDER

It is interesting just how quickly New York City history can be swept under the rug. Seemingly big events in one era become mostly forgotten side notes and trivia in another. Thousands can walk by a place daily and have no idea of the history surrounding them.

Case in point, 129 Spring Street in So-Ho. Inside this humble Federal-style townhouse is a player in one of the most sensational murders in American history. The subsequent trial brought together the most unlikely defense team; none other than Alexander Hamilton and Aaron Burr, who were never friends and eventually would become bitter rivals when Burr later shot Hamilton to death in a famous duel.

As for 129 Spring Street, it currently houses a high-end clothing store. Though it has been renovated into a sleek, modern look, downstairs is a window into another time. Behind the cash register there is a strange looking circular structure made of bricks—a seven-foot-tall well which once upon a time was center stage to one of the first "Trials of the Century."

On the night of December 22, 1799, Gulielma Elmore Sands walked out of her Greenwich Street boarding house. She was off to elope with a fellow boarder, Levi Weeks. The two had been carrying what would have then been considered a torrid affair and were trying to avoid scandal.

However, the next day, Ms. Sands was nowhere to be found. A few days later, a local boy found in the recently constructed Manhattan Well, in what was at the time Lispenard's Meadow, a muff Sands had been seen wearing earlier. On January 2, 1800,

the well was prodded with a pole, revealing her body below. An examination pointed to strangulation.

The then-small community of Manhattan was abuzz with rumors and sordid details. The coroner later confirmed that Miss Sands was pregnant. Her Quaker family ordered her body be on full display outside her boarding house so the public could see what the murderer had done to her and perhaps bolster the rumor that Weeks impregnated her.

Weeks was then put on trial for the murder. The Manhattan Well Murder as it was tagged in the press instantly became public fodder. Murder, sex before marriage and a subsequent pregnancy all made for sensational headlines in colonial New York.

Add to the fact this was the first American trial to be completely recorded by a court stenographer; the resulting transcript greatly increased popularity and interest.

Witnesses seemingly put the guilt on Weeks. Sands' cousin Catherine Sands testified that Gulielma said she was going to meet Weeks that night to wed. Several witnesses testified seeing the two acting inappropriately at the boarding house, including Richard David Croucher who perhaps had the most salacious testimony of the trial: "I saw the prisoner at the bar come out of her room, and pass the door in his shirt only, to his own room. Once too at a time, when they were less cautious than usual, I saw them in a very intimate situation." One witness also claimed seeing Weeks earlier at the well taking measurements. Others said they had seen Weeks' brother's sled near the well.

Weeks brother Ezra was a successful builder in the city and employed Levi. His brother paid for the defense, hiring lawyers Henry Brockholst Livingston, Alexander Hamilton and Aaron Burr who before their infamous duel had worked on a few cases together. It took the jury only five minutes to find Weeks not guilty, but public opinion swayed otherwise.

The murder officially remains unsolved. Levi Weeks was run out of town and settled in Natchez, Mississippi. He married, had four children, and became a successful architect and builder as well. He died in 1819 at age 49.

And of course Burr and Hamilton went on to have that dastardly duel in Weehawken, New Jersey that left Hamilton dead and Burr a pariah.

As for the well, it was sealed up and Manhattan quickly built up around it. The current house where it sits was built in 1817 and has taken on various roles in the last two hundred years, including home, restaurant, and today a clothing boutique. But very few perusing the sales racks in the little townhouse know the story of perhaps the biggest unsolved murder case in New York City history.

HAMILTON

One would have to be living under a rock to have not heard about the recent smash Broadway musical *Hamilton*. Composer, playwright and former star of the musical Lin-Manuel Miranda got the idea for the wildly successful musical after reading a book profiling Alexander Hamilton's challenging and complicated life. Miranda makes creative allusions and references to Hamilton's life by putting them to modern hip-hop music and dance. Even the Weeks trial was mentioned in the musical, helping to push the sad tale a bit back into the American consciousness.

In the musical, during the song "Non-Stop," Alexander Hamilton and Aaron Burr are at the Weeks trial and they rap to the jury, with Burr singing the line, "Our client Levi Weeks is innocent."

NEW YORK
MARBLE CEMETERY
INCORPORATED 1831

NEW YORK MARBLE CEMETERY

Incorporated 1831

ENCLOSED WITHIN THIS BLOCK IS THE OLDEST
PUBLIC NON-SECTARIAN CEMETERY IN THE CITY.
DESCENDANTS OF THE 19TH CENTURY OWNERS
MAY STILL BE BURIED HERE. THE 156 SOLID
MARBLE VAULTS WERE BUILT COMPLETELY
UNDERGROUND AS A HEALTH PRECAUTION.
THOUGH NO MARKERS ARE ON THE GROUND,
NAMES OF THE ORIGINAL OWNERS FROM EACH
FAMILY ARE ON MARBLE TABLETS IN THE
SURROUNDING WALLS. THE CEMETERY IS A
NEW YORK CITY LANDMARK AND IS ON THE
NATIONAL REGISTER OF HISTORIC PLACES.

WARNING
Falling Rocks

Old & Fragile
Stone Walls

Please
Do Not
Touch

MARBLE CEMETERY

The alleyway leading to the New York Marble Cemetery on Second Avenue near Third Street, gives just a hint of this hidden slice of lovely from the street. Located in the East Village, along the edge of the Bowery, New York Marble Cemetery's high stone walls inadvertently hide it from even locals who often too unaware of its existence. Those same walls may actually have indeed protected it from overuse and even development. It is now one of the most undisturbed plots of land in Lower Manhattan, looking less like a cemetery and more like a lush garden. It is just a half acre of land, but in a city where every square foot is precious, the space is dramatic—a true urban oasis.

In recent years the cemetery has been restored by volunteers, all of which are direct descendants of those interred here. Caroline S. DuBois, president of the board of trustees for the cemetery and a descendant herself, says, "It's wrong for your ancestor's graves to go unkempt. That's why we are here."

Even without its beauty, this historic cemetery is worthy of a visit. New York Marble Cemetery was the first non-sectarian cemetery in the city. Founded in 1830 by Perkins Nichols, it was developed as a commercial enterprise, during the era when the first descendants of the American Revolution generation were becoming upwardly mobile

and successful. Many were manufacturers, builders, bankers, and other occupations congruent with an emerging society, thus able to afford more affluent possessions like family crypts. Social norms were also loosening up a bit. Episcopalians were marrying Presbyterians (gasp!) and so on.

Also during this time, contagious diseases were ravaging large urban areas. Lower Manhattan was particularly hit hard by yellow fever and cholera. Desperate to control the outbreaks, the city resorted to banning earthen burials below Canal Street. Fear at the time was that vapors from the bodies would seep through the ground and infect the living. To work around the no burial ban, the Marble Cemetery was built with underground stone vaults. The result is a wide open space with no headstones. Instead stone family plaques made of Tuckahoe marble are embedded in the surrounding walls.

The 156 stone arched vaults are situated in 6 orderly columns from front to back, ten feet below the ground. From 1830 to 1870 the majority of internments took place with the last occurring in 1937. In all, over 2,100 persons have been buried here, though the number has reduced dramatically over the decades. It is because often during the last part of the 19th Century, families of the departed often wanted their loved ones to rest in a more fashionable place. Therefore about a quarter of the people buried here were reinterred in Green-Wood in Brooklyn, Woodland Cemetery in The Bronx or Sleepy Hollow Cemetery in Westchester County, New York.

Notable people laid to rest at New York Marble Cemetery include the chief engineer of the Erie Canal, Benjamin Wright, New York Mayor Aaron Clark and the father of publisher Charles Schribner. Family names familiar with many New Yorkers include the Varick's, Hoyt's and Beekman's.

New York Marble Cemetery's unusual location and rare pastoral setting in the heart of the East Village has given it a renewed life and purpose in the 21st century. The grounds are rented out for many events including weddings, film shoots even fashion shows. Money earned from the rentals goes to the cemetery's upkeep and restoration. But the trustees have had to turn down a few rather unusual requests. One couple wanted to have a Friday the 13th wedding. Film companies will also occasionally ask to use the vaults (which are sealed closed) if they can film underground. "We of course said 'Uh, no' to those requests, our ancestors our down there," says Caroline.

The cemetery has a welcoming feel to it. "We want it to be a happy place", says she says. People come here not only to peruse the stone plaques but also to sunbath, rest, read, some even bring their dogs, on a leash of course.

There are a couple of ways to see the cemetery for yourself. At certain times of the year, it is opened for the public once of month usually the fourth Sunday.

The other way is a bit more expensive. Two of the vaults recently went up for sale for $350,000 each. The good news is it is capable of holding many family members.

Caroline herself says she and other trustees will be laid to rest here eventually in their families' vaults.

Though the cemetery is close to her heart because of her family connection, she says its important to everyone, "What makes a city special is the layers and lay-ers of history. The more people are aware of the history around them, the more they care about their neighborhood. It is a circle of protection."

THE OTHER MARBLE CEMETERY

Understandably it is a bit confusing, but within a stone's throw of the New York Marble Cemetery is the New York City Marble Cemetery. Still confused? Not the New York, but New York *CITY* Marble Cemetery.

The reason for the confusion stems from the popularity of the New York Marble Cemetery when it first opened in 1830. A second one was almost immediately planned and opened just a year later. Both cemeteries are completely independent of each other.

They do however have a few similarities. Both have Tuckahoe marble vaults underground, but at the second cemetery also has many headstones above ground giving it a more traditional cemetery look and feel.

Notable people who were buried here include three former mayors, Stephen Allen, (who was also NY Governor) Isaac Varian and Marinus Willet, some Roosevelt ancestors including James Henry Roosevelt who founded Roosevelt Hospital and archaeologist John Lloyd Stevens who spe-cialized in the Mayan culture. His monument has an exquisite Mayan glyph motif on front.

The cemetery once even held the remains of the fifth president of the United States—James Monroe. In 1831, he died while living with his daughter due to his ongoing financial problems. In 1856, Virginia Governor Henry A. Wise raised funds to reinter Monroe in his native state of Vir-ginia where he now rests in Hollywood Cemetery in Richmond.

MURRAY'S CHEESE CAVES

Murray's Cheese has been a Greenwich Village mainstay since 1940, when it began as a humble egg and butter shop selling cheese on the side. Today they offer a broad variety of cheeses from around the world making it one of the largest cheese stores in the United States.

But longtime customers may not even realize Murray's does not just import and sell cheese. They are also makers and connoisseurs, often creating many of their own varieties. Like fine wine, they carefully age cheese themselves in a most delicate and deliberate manner so that they can offer a unique and superior selection. Aging in their own "cheese caves" or aging facilities which provide just the right surroundings for the product to age to its peak flavor.

These aging facilities harken back to a time when European cheesemakers used actual caves to preserve and age cheese. The constant cool, humid air in caves provide bacterial cultures just the right environment for the process. Today Murray's is one of just a handful of places in the United States with these specialized aging facilities. Visually Murray's caves may not have the quaint picturesque quality of their naturally-formed French counterparts, but they make it up in performance and consistency.

Located in the rather industrial section of Long Island City, Queens there are four caves and one drying room, all with varying environments. They include the washed rind cave, bloomy rind cave, natural rind cave and alpine cave. Each is calibrated with different mold cultures, temperatures and moisture controlled by a spray humidifier.

Upon entering each concrete enclosed room, one is hit with distinctively different aroma. Just like the cheeses, one cave will have a pungent smell, while another can have a more subtle scent due to the variety of elements.

One of the major advantages of Murray's caves is cheese can be aged often within miles of where it will be enjoyed. And just like any other perishable food, cheese shipped from another region can over-ripen by the time it reaches consumers. Therefore

Murray's Cheese will ship unripened cheese from places like Vermont, Colorado, and as far away as France and Italy. Then depending on the type of cheese, they will finish the aging process themselves in their own cheese caves.

The caves are rarely opened for tours and are mostly for industry folk. If one is lucky enough to visit, be ready for a thorough decontamination process. Everyone must wear lab coats, rubber boots, hairnets, and, if necessary, beardnets. Hands must

be washed then spritzed with hand sanitizer as an extra precaution. Rubber boots are dipped in a foot bath to assure no contaminants enter the cheese caves. All of it

well worth the trouble considering how controlled the microbial ecosystem is in each of these caves. And well appreciated for all those who love great cheese.

MUSEUM OF NATURAL HISTORY SACKLER INSTITUTE

The American Museum of Natural History not only can boast to being one of the largest museums in the world, but it also world-renowned for it scientific research. Their research and studies cover some 3.5 billion years of history of nature and mankind.

While the public marvels at their wonderful displays and specimens in the exhibition halls, researchers and scientists affiliated with the museum are participating in over 100 in house research and out in the field expeditions worldwide every year.

And with the revolutionary strides taken in genetic research in recent years, it is only fitting the museum is moving itself to the forefront of the genetic revolution. Since 2001, the museum's Sackler Institute for Comparative Genomics has been the museum's next step forward in this discipline. It is called "conservation genetics," the Sackler Institute is an animal gene repository. One of the largest in the country, its purpose is to give researchers and scientists around the world access to DNA and RNA through biological samples of different species of animals. Ultimately millions of samples will be available for study.

This fascinating area of research is rarely seen by regular museum goers, it is tucked away in one of the least auspicious places of the museum. Just to get to the institute one must (with a museum associate of course) traipse past the regular exhibitions through a couple of backrooms. The trail becomes seemingly cold as one is led through what appears to be the museum's workshop, to which a pair of very nondescript doors look to be no more than entrance to a utility closet. On the other side is Sackler's state of the art laboratory.

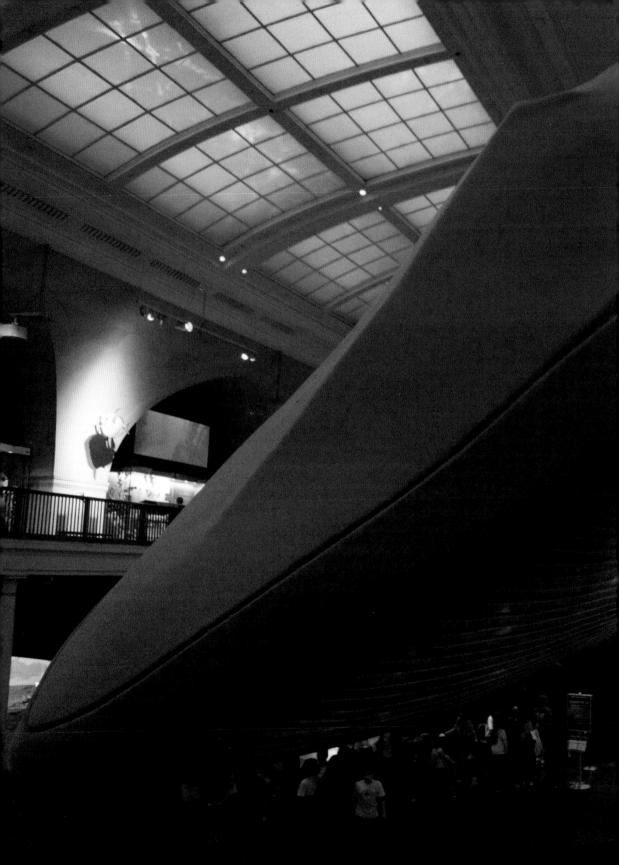

Instead of jars of pickled specimens or taxidermied animals, visitors are greeted by eight enormous cryogenic vats holding the tissue specimens. Inside the containers are over 100,000 and counting tissue, hair, and blood samples from a variety of animals from around the world.

But before you get any fantastical ideas of the American Museum of Natural History becoming *Jurassic Park* or *Night at the Museum* having a new ending, cloning is out of the question, these samples are used for practical, real research, some of which is already being put to use today.

Take for instance the lowly space bedbug. Researchers were able to take samples and break down the insect's entire genome. With that information, they were able to, among other things, find out which genes make the bedbugs resistant to insecticides.

The specimens are helping the species own too. Bat RNA samples are being used to figure out new ways of stopping white nose syndrome in bats. Since 2006, the fungal disease has killed off over five and a half million bats in North America.

The Sackler Institute receives its samples from a variety of sources. For instance,

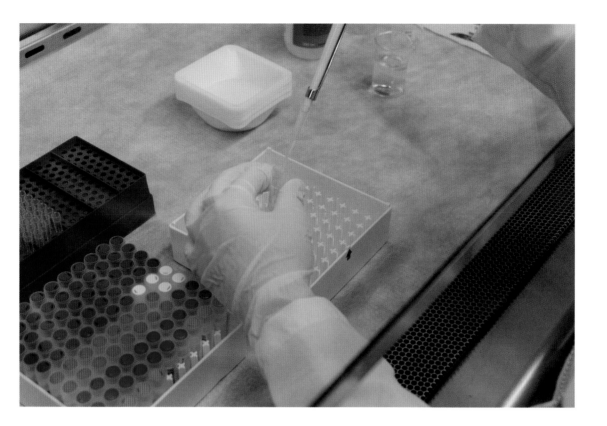

the U.S. Park Service provides samples of species native to parks under their jurisdiction. Some of those samples are being used to find new ways to help endangered animals like the island fox on California's Channel Islands.

Many of the samples are taken in the field by trained individuals, non-invasively, without harm to the animal.

With samples coming in on a steady basis, the cryogenic vats at the institute are capable of storing over one million tissue samples.

The vats keep the samples cool in a seemingly low tech way but it is very efficient. Eight inches of liquid nitrogen is placed or "charged" in the bottom of each vat, as the liquid nitrogen pool evaporates it creates a -256°F environment. It is so efficient at keeping the samples cool, what little electricity is spent is mostly for the vats diagnostic gauges. The vats are even capable of keeping the samples sufficiently frosty for 30 days without even being touched.

The animal samples are simply placed in racks which rest inside the vats. When a sample is requested, barcodes on each sample tube are linked to a computer database. Samples distributed are only about the size of a pinhead, assuring plenty of samples will be available for generations to come.

THEODORE ROOSEVELT ROTUNDA AND MEMORIAL HALL

There is good reason the main entrance is named after the 26th President of the United States. Theodore Roosevelt was not only an avid outdoorsman and conservationist, but his ties to the Museum of Natural History run deep. His father, Theodore Roosevelt Sr., actually helped found the museum and even had the charter signed in 1869 at the family home on East 20th Street.

As a youth, the younger Roosevelt learned taxidermy from one of naturalist John James Audubon's taxidermists and began contributing animals specimens to the museum in 1872. One of his specimens, a snowy owl, is on display in Memorial Hall.

Future president and distant cousin, Franklin D. Roosevelt, laid the cornerstone for the two story memorial in 1937. During the dedication he told the crowd that Theodore had said to him, "Franklin, you can learn more about nature and life in the museum than in all the books and schools in the world."

The dinosaur skeletons in the Roosevelt Rotunda are perhaps the most well known exhibit in the museum. It depicts a Barosaurus protecting its young from an Allosaurus. The skeletons are actually cast replicas because displaying them in this dramatic manner would be too heavy for the actual fossils.

NYPL TREASURES

Bryant Park is a quiet repose from Midtown's daily madness. Its wide expansive lawn is always full of sunbathers, workers on their lunch break, and tourists resting their feet. In the winter the park transforms into a holiday wonderland complete with skating ring.

But few know that as they sprawled out on the green, perhaps reading a favorite author, they are literally on top of some of the greatest works of mankind. For six floor underground are vaults used by the main branch of The New York City Public Library.

Only second to the Library of Congress in the United States, and fourth in the world in terms of items held, the NYPL has some 53 million throughout its five borough library system. Space is obviously of the essence for the library, it makes sense they would try to utilize every space they can.

During the library's 1989 renovation, the park was closed off, and 30 feet was dug out to build the vault. It houses 40 miles of the 125 miles of shelving. Space is even more utilized by using a compact shelving system which allows for the shelves to move together, thus creating more space. In all, some 3 million books are stored there alone.

It is just one of the five vaults at the library since it was first opened in 1911. Some of the vaults under the main library even help to give the massive main building its strength. Below cast iron shelves also work as structural points and are left in place even if they are not being used for books.

Part of all the need for this space is because the main branch is not a lending library. Rather books must be used within the library. Also the public cannot pull the

Edna Barnes Salomon Room
316

McGraw Rotunda

books off the shelves themselves, rather a catalogue worker retrieves it for them. This is where the stacks system in the vaults really comes into place. The procedure has been used for decades and is a marvel of old and new technology.

One writes the call number of the book they want on a call slip, the slips are sorted then sent to various stack areas where catalogers find the requested books, and the books are put onto a conveyor belt to the waiting person. The whole exchange can take only twenty minutes. Up until 2011 the library used its original pneumatic tubes system to ferry the slips back and forth to the catalogers. The beloved system was retired because acquiring replacement tube capsules became too difficult.

With millions of items cataloged, the NYPL has acquired quite its share of interesting, unusual, if not downright treasures over the decades.

They include a copy of the Gutenberg Bible, which is the first consequential printed book in Western civilization and helped usher in the movable type age. Only 48 copies survive. Also there is an original copy of *A Christmas Carol*, which was author Charles Dickens' personal copy. It is called called a "prompt-copy" used by Dickens during his public readings. The book is a treasure trove for scholars and fans alike for it is filled with his own personal notations and cues.

The library even has some of the earliest known forms of writing. Found on Cuneiform tablets from ancient Mesopotamia from the 3rd-2nd millennium, they are clay tablets with baked impressions in clay. Though historic, the samples are rather mundane in their context; they include bookkeeping items such as: inventory, payroll, and barter or exchange rates.

Presidential possessions include Thomas Jefferson's autographed copy of the Declaration of Independence and George Washington's personal recipe for beer from 1757.

Perhaps the most beloved, if not cherished, items in the library are not books but rather toys. They are the actual dolls Christopher Milne were given as a boy. Not ringing a bell? Perhaps his middle name will help—Robin. Yes, Christopher Robin was a real boy and his father A. A. Milne wrote the famous stories around his son's dolls, Winnie the Pooh and friends. They were donated to the library in 1987.

LIONS

It would be hard to find two statues in New York City not more well-known and beloved. The New York City Public Library lions have been standing guard at the stairs of the library since 1911. They are without a doubt the very symbol of the New York Public Library which has even copyrighted the pair and are used as the library's logo.

Many people do not know they actually have names too. After a few nicknames over the years, Mayor Fiorello LaGuardia declared in the 1930s the two lions will be ever name as Patience on the left and Fortitude on the right. An apt name for the time, they were qualities New Yorkers needed during The Great Depression.

The lions were no cheap after thought or quick undertaking when the library was built. They were sculpted under the recommendation of renowned American sculptor, Augustus Saint-Gaudens. Artist Edward Clark Peter was paid the princely sum of $8,000 to actually design them

and an additional $5,000 was required to have them carved by the Piccirilli Brothers out of pink Tennessee marble.

In some ways the two lions have been loved to death. For decades tradition was to dress the lions up for holidays and events. But items like wreaths around their necks for Christmas and baseball caps on top of their heads for the World's Series along with the elements have made the lions eroded and worn. After a 2014 assessment and restoration, the lions are faring better but for now on will be handled with a gentler touch.

P. E. GUERIN

Jane Street is a quintessential Greenwich Village street, a quiet enclave of small townhouses and apartment buildings, but among them is a wonderful vestige of "Old New York" manufacturing. A metal foundry which has been making its products here since the 19th century.

P. E. Guerin is a decorative hardware company specializing in a variety of items like doorknobs, faucets, and hinges. But these are not typical big box chainstore buy-them-by-the-box items. Rather they are exquisite, individually handcrafted, pieces often referred to as "jewelry for the home." Customers have included the Plaza Hotel, Henry Ford, the Waldorf-Astoria Hotel, and almost all the buildings designed by famed architects McKim, Meade, and White.

Incredibly the company has been making its wares in the same building on Jane Street since 1892. Enter their front door and one is immediately aware of how this is truely a one of a kind place. Start with their showroom lined with Victorian-era display cabinets showing off thousands of their products. Careful not to disturb any of the three cats who have a run of the place. These unofficial employees can be found loung-ing around the hardware in between their mouse hunting duties.

In the back is the catalog room, where thousands of templates, casting models, and catalogs are stored. Incredibly, a customer can pull out a catalog from whatever year, say 1903, pick out an item and a craftsperson is able to make the exact item from scratch.

Styles run the gamut: victorian, art nouveau, art deco, etc. . . . Customers can also bring in their own design to have fabricated. Custom pieces are sometimes incorporated with a family coat of arms or even a likeness of a favorite pet.

P. E. Guerin was founded by its namesake in 1857. A French immigrant, Pierre Emmanuel Guerin ran the business at a series of locations before settling on Jane Street. Now not only is the building the same, but ownership is in the same family, run now by Mr. Guerin's great-grand nephew Andrew Ward. Tradition runs deep with their employees too; many of them have worked here for decades.

All the work is done on three floors in various departments. The workshops have an old-world craftsmen look.

The company is one of the only businesses in the world still doing it the "hard way." Their fabrication process is intricate, labor-intensive, and expensive. However their products rarely need to be replaced, are not mass produced and often appreciate in value.

Many are indeed surprised as to just how much work goes into making an item. It is a process unchanged in over 100 years because the quality cannot be matched through automation.

The first step is to locate the original hardware from the archives. A mold of it is then created from sand then it is baked for several hours. Various metals are melted in a blast furnace crucible to create molten brass. At one point the crucible heats to 2,000°F—so hot it casts a green flame. The crucible of molten brass is lifted out of the furnace and ever so carefully poured into the molds. After only a few minutes the metal has cooled enough to be broken out of its molds. What is left is a somewhat rough piece that goes through a series of brushings, cuttings, and polishings to get the piece closer to its desired shape and texture. Next the pieces are dipped in acid to get rid of scaling. It is then back to a worker who cleans and files the surfaces even more.

Next, the item is put in the hands of a chaser craftsperson, who is able to really actuate the piece. Because so many of the detailing is lost in the casting and filing processes, the chaser's job is to redelineate parts of the design back into the piece. With little hammers and chisels the chaser is in a way sculpting the metal by moving and shaping it. It is these details that set P. E. Guerin's work above the rest.

Why go to all the fuss and expense for something so utilitarian? Vice President of the company Martin Grubman puts it

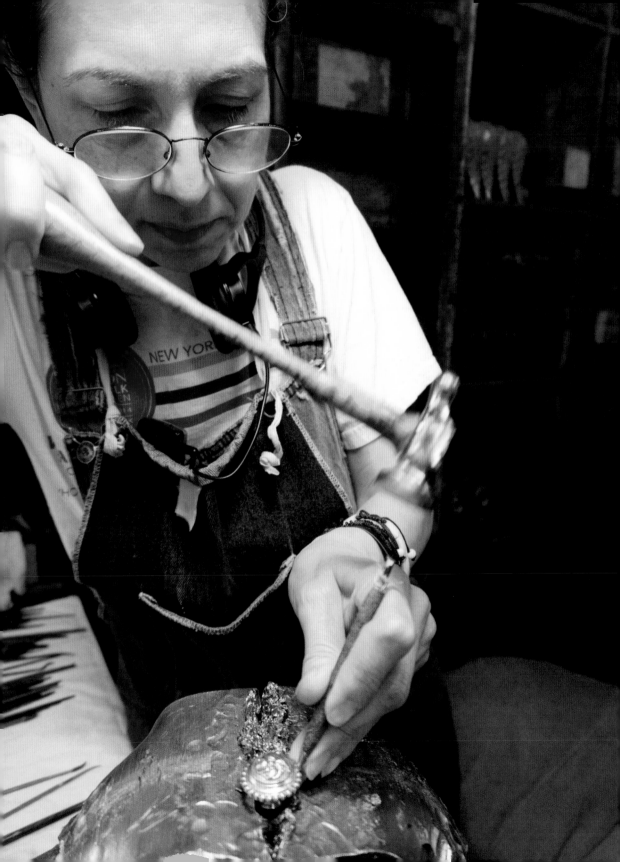

succinctly, "It's not just the beauty, it is the kind of thing that is tactile. It is the faucet you turn on when you brush your teeth, the doorknob that you turn daily, the thing that makes you smile every time you touch it. So why wouldn't you want the best?"

JANE STREET

There is something about Jane Street that attracts creative types. Just five blocks long, this street most likely had more artists who have lived here per capita than any other street in the city. Sometimes referred to as "Authors' Row" the list is exhaustive. Just a sampling includes John Cheever, Bobe Mayse, Susan Brownmiller, and Mary Louise Wilson. And this does not even include all the short story writers, journalists, and of course the undiscovered. So if you're looking for artistic inspiration, Jane Street might be worth a stroll.

THE PLAYERS

The Players was born partly out of a national tragedy, and after over 125 years the club is still successful at what it was created to do: bring people together. The core purpose of The Players was to be a meeting place for actors and non-actors alike to share their love of the arts, particularly the theatre. As one of the oldest private clubs in New York City, incredibly it is still in its original location layered with artistic treasures.

Founded in 1888, The Players was the inspiration of actor Edwin Booth, perhaps the most prolific and famous actor of his time. Always concerned with the negative stereotypes brought against his profession, Booth tried fervently to get his fellow thespians to interact with non-actors. As The Players curator Raymond Wemmlinger says, "They were more akin to circus folk of the time. Women in the theatre in many circles were one step above prostitutes."

When Booth's brother John Wilkes Booth assassinated President Abraham Lincoln in 1865, Edwin was not only determined to salvage his family's name, but also the world of theatre. (John Wilkes was also an actor.) So he created The Players for actors to interact with the outside world. He wanted to bring lovers of the arts—be it theatre, music, literature, or fine arts—professionals and non, together for kinship and understanding. "We do not mingle enough with minds that influence the world," Booth said of his fellow actors, "We should measure ourselves through personal contact with

outsiders . . . I want my club to be a place where actors are away from the glamour of the theatre."

So dedicated to the idea, Booth purchased the townhouse at 16 Gramercy Park South for $75,000 and gifted it to the newly created club. The Greek Revival home had been built in 1845 for banker Elihu Townsend. Booth hired fellow Players member, famed architect Stanford White to renovate the place. Inside his distinctive touches are seen throughout the space with much of the originality of the place today still intact.

Even the outside is original, with extra-large gas lanterns—some of the oldest in the city.

Opening on New Year's Eve in 1888, original Players members included Mark Twain and General William Tecumseh Sherman. Over the years members have included John Barrymore, Dwight Eisenhower, Nikola Tesla, Christopher Plummer, Liza Minnelli, Walter Cronkite, Ethan Hawke, Helen Hayes and the list goes on and on. Member and late-night talk show host Jimmy Fallon has even hosted his annual Christmas parties here.

SARAH BERNHARDT ROOM

The club was men only until 1989, but that did not stop the club from celebrating and hosting woman. In 1911, they honored actress Sarah Bernhardt for her theatrical achievements. During the evening she managed to get stuck in a malfunctioning elevator for an hour. Afterwards she served tea. Her presence is still felt here, the elevator has ever since been playful known now as the "Sarah Bernhardt" room, complete with her likeness adoring the inside.

A walkthrough The Players is akin to strolling through the history of American theatre. Their rooms are full of wonderful portraits of actors, some done by well-known artists like Norman Rockwell and William Glackens. There are also props, costumes and other theatre ephemera on display from of several generations. Everything has a wonderful tale or origin. There are Edwin Booth's original Shakespearian costumes used during his famous stage tours, death masks of prominent thespians, and even Mark Twain's pool stick (not to mention the pool table he played on).

The most fascinating place in The Players is also the most private; Edwin Booth's personal upstairs apartment which he called his, "Nest among the treetops of Gramercy." Incredibly the space has been kept exactly the way it was when he died in 1893 at age 59. Proof is the stale hint of tobacco smoke still slightly permeating in the space. There is a patina rarely seen or felt in other period rooms. His personal possessions do not seem neatly arranged for viewing rather they have an authentic lived in look. Perhaps the most intriguing item is a human skull. It was said to be given to Booth's father Junius

Brutus Booth, also an actor, who once shared a jail cell with a horse thief named Fontaine. Before the man was hanged for his crimes he asked for his skull be sent to Junius for used in performances of the play Hamlet. Edwin did actually use it in his performances and the skull is engraved with the inscription, "And the rest is silence."

But with all these wonderful artifacts, The Players is hardly a museum, rather a lively social club with regular events and services. The kitchen is open for members and their guests on a daily basis serving lunch and dinner. Though the club is for members and their guests, The Players extensive theatrical library hosts a wealth of archival information including original plays and manuscripts.

So even today, the club holds a reverent respect to its past, but a robust social calendar mixing fans of the arts and those who create them just like Mister Booth would have liked.

POMANDER WALK

Residents of Pomander Walk are used to it; a group of passerbys peering through the security gate with almost incredulous looks on their faces. Who can blame them? For it is a wonderfully curious sight. For just beyond the gates is seemingly picturesque European village. A tiny enclave of cottages somehow managing to exist among the concrete and steel of Manhattan. As author and former resident Darryl Pinckney said of Pomander Walk in his book *High Cotton*, The place "an insertion of incredible whimsy" into the Upper West Side.

It lays just off of 94th and 95th streetsbetween Broadway and West End Avenue, on an elevated patch of land of two-story cottages situated in two rows. Each one looking fussed over and loved, with front flowerbeds carefully manicured and fronts brightly painted in primary color hues.

Actually Pomander was never supposed to be permanent or frankly, this cherished. It was initially built in 1921 to earn some fast cash for a larger real estate project. Its builder, Thomas J. Healy who ran a series of businesses including nightclubs and cafes initially wanted to build a hotel here. But when funding fell through, he built Pomander Walk as a rental complex to generate some income. Once he raised enough money, he planned to tear down the little houses and build the hotel. However the plan never came into fruition, with Healy dying in 1927.

His inspiration to build Pomander Walk like a sleepy English village comes from the world of theatre. Initially he wanted to rent to people working in theatre. So he took the little colony straight from the set of a popular Broadway play, *Pomander Walk*, named after a fictional walkway in the London suburb of Chiswick. Written by Louis N. Parker, the romantic comedy (which was a novel before it was a play) revolves around a "keeping up with the Jones'" plot, thus the small, yet grand homes were a fitting analogy for the play. As Parker stated in a 1921 *New York Times* interview, "The little houses," says Louis N. Parker, "were built in the sober and staid style introduced during the reign of her Majesty Queen Anne. The architect had taken a slyly humorous delight in making them miniature copies of much more pretentious town mansions." You might have thought the houses were meant to be inhabited by very small Dukes, so stately were they in their own way."

Built by the architect firm King and Campbell, the houses are built from a variety of brick and stucco with some half-timbering decoration all contributing to the overall Tudor-revival style—a style quite in vogue in New York City during the 1920s. The interiors are plain and simple, though today's residents, like all other New Yorker's, have learned to maximize and decorate the spaces to the hilt. Most have converted the houses from two family to one family homes giving each around 1,300 square feet of living space. Though modernization has been undertaken, like proper wiring, kitchens, and bathrooms, original touches like window boxes, wrought iron railings, and curb gardens have all been respectfully preserved.

As the decades came and went, Pomander Walk remained a rental property and slowly went into disrepair. Luckily it was landmarked in 1982 and turned into a co-op with most of the owners dedicated to improving and preserving the homes.

Becoming a resident in Pomander Walk is not easy. The vetting process was once particularly hard, but now the homes themselves are restrictive. They can go for upwards of a couple of million dollars—not bad for houses said to cost a little under three-thousand dollars to build. These homes are so loved and cherished, they are even known to be passed down to family members and friends.

If Pomander Walk seems like country living in the middle of a metropolis, resident Brelyn Vandenberg agrees, "During the summer the doors swing open and stay that way. My kids can go outside and play out in the front, and I can cook dinner while I watch them." Natalie Weiss, a former resident and real estate broker who has sold several houses here, says Pomander Way is a way of life, "Because of the proximity of everyone, you have to be friendly. It makes people good neighbors."

ACTORS

Healy's plan to attract artistic types worked; better than he probably imagined. Throughout its history, Pomander has attracted all kinds of artists including movie director William Parke, playwright Herbert Stoddard, and actors Nancy Carroll, Ward Morehouse, Herbert Stothart, Paulette Goddard, and Rosalind Russell. Humphrey Bogart was rumored to have lived here a short time as a young man. Even today there are at least a couple of working actors living here. Pomander Walk itself has hit the silver screen; scenes from the Woody Allen movie, *Hannah and Her Sisters* were shot here.

PRATT STEAM PLANT

Brooklyn's Pratt Institute has a distinguished and noble history. Always on the forefront culturally and politically, it is one of the first colleges in the United States to be all inclusive regardless of race, gender or socio-economic background. Its Clinton Hill neighborhood campus is one of the most picturesque in the nation, dripping with Victorian-era charm. So beautiful, the private campus is open during the daytime to the public as a pass-through for pedestrian traffic. Along with the historic buildings here is a little known living, breathing piece of history from the American industrial revolution.

It is the oldest running steam-powered electric plant privately owned in the country. Located in campus' East Building in a two tier plant engine room, the myriad of steel and iron is a throwback to when steam powered America, but this is by no means just a museum piece.

Over the decades the steam plant has held a wide variety of jobs at the school. Besides heating, the plant has provided incandescent and arc lighting for the campus and provided power for the machine shops through a belt system. The plant still does its fair share of work at the school, generating electrical power and helping to heat campus buildings during the winter.

The machinery is a visual marvel just to watch. The massive machines move and churn more gracefully and seemingly better than their modern counterparts. Mirror-shine pistons glistening with lubricant push and pull as the smell of steam wafts through the air. Along with the age appropriate old-fashioned dial and massive flywheels, the place is a rarified sight. Though closed to the public, art students from the school regularly sketch the machinery, and the steam plant is a must stop on the campus tour for prospective students.

Incredibly just four chief engineers have overseen the plant since it was built in 1887.

But the intriguing visuals do not end in the steam plant. The plant's workshop has parts and tools everywhere, looking like an incredible archive or perhaps repository for industrial revolution parts and knowhow. Though monumentally cluttered, one can sense the caretaker knows where everything is and its purpose.

Not surprisingly because of the steam machines' age, spare parts are nearly impossible to find. Caretakers of the steam plant have gotten quite adept at fashioning the parts on their own. Over the years the plant has also been accumulating quite a collection of different steam-powered whistles from old locomotives to the famed ship, SS *Normandie*. For years on New Year's Eve, the whistles would be hooked together in unison then blown at midnight to usher in the New Year to deafening shrieks.

MAIN LIBRARY

One of the more impressive buildings on the Pratt's campus is the Main Library, designed in 1896 by renowned New York architect William Tubby in a Victorian-Renaissance Revival style. Inside are wonderfully ornate Victorian era interiors designed and made by Tiffany Glass and Decorations Company. They feature original book brackets and wood shelving designed with elaborate and ornate flourishes. Today the library has been carefully restored and painted with its original vibrant colors.

The main library is another point of pride in Pratt's list of firsts. It was Brooklyn's first free public library not only open to students but also to the public.

RADIO CITY ROXY APARTMENT

Radio City has been called the "showplace of the nation." The largest indoor theatre in the world, it held more than seven-hundred movie premieres including the original versions of *King Kong* and *National Velvet*. Able to seat upwards of 6,000 people, the lavish venue has hosted everyone from Frank Sinatra to Britney Spears and of course the world famous Radio City Rockettes precision dance troupe.

Radio City Music Hall is anything but ordinary. In all, more than 300 million people have come through its doors. The entertainment venue is perhaps the pinnacle of Art Deco motif, emanating the over the top grandeur and opulence of the age with the largest curtain in the world and its marquee taking up a whole city block,

But with all those visitors, few get to see one of the true gems of at Radio City, a space as grand as any part of the venue and another Art Deco gem, one of the last truly original interiors of its kind preserved the way it was meant to be.

Known as the Roxy Suite, it was built for Samuel "Roxy" Rothafel a live theatre impresario who oversaw the building of Radio City Hall. The Rockefeller family who financed the project had the special apartment built here as a gift to Rothafel for all his hard work. Roxy was multi-talented in the theatre world, helping troubled theaters across the country bring in audiences. He also planned new venues and was even the creator of the Rockettes, which started in a theatre in Missouri. Working with Architect

AUTOGRAPH BOOK

A wonderful curio inside the Roxy Suite is an autograph book which is part of a tradition going back to when Radio City opened in 1932. Every performer who has graced Radio City's stage has signed one of these guest books. There are thirteen large sized folios filled with performer's autographs and sometimes a notation or two. The one currently on display at the Roxy Suite is actually a facsimile with a sampling of some of the more interesting autographs collected over the years.

Edward Durrell Stone and interior designer Donald Deskey, Roxy got Radio City's cruise ship motif idea when he set sail to Europe looking for ideas for the theatre.

Radio City opened in 1932, but unfortunately Roxy died in 1936 so the apartment was used little by him. A terrible shame because Deskey spared no expense in his design. Like the rest of Radio City, he utilized the latest in materials including Bakelite, Aluminum and Permatex.

The fifth floor apartment is wrapped in art deco trappings. The 20-foot-high ceilings are covered in lacquered cherrywood, creating a dramatic space along with an outdoor balcony. All of the furniture was designed specifically for the apartment, giving it even more of a one-of-a-kind feel and resonance with smart lines, unapologetic colors, and prominent geometric shapes throughout.

In the back of the apartment is the dining area, the most unique part of an already unforgettable apartment. The circular space is topped off with a dome ceiling; the idea was to create good acoustics for conversation. Interestingly there are no straight lines in there either. Doors are curved along the wall, which led to a kitchen.

Luckily the beauty of the place is seen by some today. The apartment is sometimes used as a green room for visiting performers—Paul McCartney and Elton John among others. It is also sometimes leased out for private events and is a stop on the Back Stage tour at Radio City Music Hall. Roxy, who was known for being very social, would be pleased.

ROOFTOP HOUSE

The old adage "New York City does not work around you, you work around it" is a stark reality most locals have had to experience. Whether trying to find an apartment larger than a walk-in closet, or a career not requiring a least a 60-hour workweek, New York City can indeed sometimes seem daunting. But little by little, each person carves out their own niche here.

David Puchkoff and his wife Eileen Stukane, who live in the West Village, went one step further; building and planting their own Shangri-La, a little country cottage complete with a meadow all situated on their apartment building rooftop.

During a weekend trip to the Endless Mountains in Pennsylvania, David had an epiphany. While rowing in front of his friends' lakeside cottage, he saw the wooden-railed porch, shuttered windows, and warm gathering of friends, and thought: "This is what I want. I can't have the lakeside view, but I can have a porch that looks like it belongs in the country."

They began to build their wonderful oasis in 2002. David says building the 300-square-foot cottage and 1,200-square-foot meadow was not as difficult as it might seem. Of course, living on the top floor of their co-op building, obviously helped, but putting up the wooden clapboard bungalow and porch was pretty straightforward. To unify the living space with the rooftop cottage, they constructed a staircase from their existing apartment leading to the upstairs addition.

Creating the meadow was a bit more challenging. It takes no imagination to realize that putting vegetation which requires constant watering is just asking for trouble. Working with green rooftop vegetation specialists, they first prepared the roof with various liner materials, waterproofing the roof and protecting it from soil and roots. One innovation was a subfloor of miniature cuplike plastic receptacles to retain rain water while still supplying it to vegetation. About 6 inches of top soil was applied to the roof surface after checking with a structural engineer.

From there David and Eileen created their cityscape meadow by using succulents and sedums. These desert plants turned out to be the perfect fit for they thrive in shallow soil and require a minimal amount of water, which they are able to naturally store for long periods. In all, David and Eileen planted some 2,500 plants in the space. In winter some of the plants, like the blooming cacti, are moved onto the porch, which they enclose in customized plastic to create a seasonal greenhouse thanks in part to the heat emanating up at night from their apartment below and the natural warmth from the sun in the day.

Seeing the beautiful roof-top oasis begs the question: "Why are there not more of these in the city?" The small cottage porch with its front meadow creates a wonderfully serene atmosphere. There is indeed a unique feeling when opening up the screen door and walking onto their wooden porch to sweeping views of Manhattan. "It's a sense of unreality. You think you are in the country, you're on a porch, there's green all around you, hear birds, but you look up and you're in the city," David says.

Besides their friends and family, some of the biggest fans of this spot are the many birds who stopover to forage and even nest here. Ants, ladybugs, butterflies and bees have also made their way up to the rooftop, perhaps to see what all the fuss is about.

Of course being a private residence, the public is out of luck in getting a look-see. (Let's be honest, would you want someone knocking your door to see your living arrangements?) Still David is kind enough to always answer questions he gets from people who stumble on the place either seeing it on the internet or spying it from another building, knowing he has something special. And the best reward? David says: "You don't feel like we have to leave the city, we have our own getaway here."

PATCHIN PLACE

Walking down the crooked streets of Greenwich Village, it is easy to spot little pieces of 19th century New York peeking through. Be it boot scrapers embedded in the front stoop of a handsome townhouse or cobblestones emerging through worn asphalt, these little finds are an immediate connection to the past.

Take Patchin Place for instance, where at the very end of this private dead end alley on West 10th Street and 6th Avenue is a simple street light. Not impressive on first look, but it is the last original gas cast iron street lamp in the city. Although it is now lit by a compact fluorescent bulb, it can still boast about being the oldest public operating street light in the city.

Lamps like these had a short lifespan in the city. Most were installed in the 1860s then fairly quickly became useless as electricity made its way through New York in the 1880s.

There are parts of the city which still have have gas lamps running by flame. Many can be seen in Midtown's Murray Hill and in Greenwich Village. But they are not owned or operated by the city, rather grandfathered in so residents can run them off their own gas lines and are sometimes reproductions of the originals.

Patchin Place is also notable for having some well-known writers live here over the years, too, including e. e. cummings and Theodore Dreiser.

ST. AUGUSTINE SLAVE GALLERY

New Yorkers pride themselves on their diversity and inclusion. So it can be jarring for some to learn their city was once a center in America's slave trade. In fact at one point, New York's slave owners had more than any other state north of Virginia. Emancipation of slaves came to the state in 1827, but not surprisingly, Jim Crow type laws languished in the state for decades.

On the Lower East Side in Manhattan, there is a little church with a rare and unusual artifact of that time, virtually forgotten for decades, but now thoughtfully preserved.

It can be found at St. Augustine of Hippo Episcopal Church on Henry Street, a sturdy stone Greek Revival church typical of early 19th-Century. Tiny wooden pews are neatly packed throughout the nave and there is an original Henry Erben organ in back—said to be the oldest in America.

Just to the sides of the organ pipes on the second floor is evidence of America's slave holding past and perhaps a reminder of how far we have come as a nation. They are the slave galleries, one of a very few still in existence.

The rooms are sparse, merely open balconies. Inside are roughly hewn, bare bleacher-like benches. The room provides an up close and personal view, albeir a small one, to the harsh realities faced by the occupants. More akin to squatting than sitting, the benches are low and hardly comfortable. Moreover, the heat is stifling, there is no cross ventilation, and the windows cannot be open. Add a large group of people and

one can only imagine how unpleasant the simple, pious act of going to church must have been. Parishioner and church historian, Minnie Curry, ponders: "Can you imagine, farming in the morning, then perhaps rowing across the river from Brooklyn, then sitting up here for church? That took a lot of faith to do so."

St. Augustine's has done something simple but wonderful with the space: they left it alone. Other than painting and patching the walls for protective measures, there is little alteration. The heat, the benches with their marked, scarred and stained wood, all add to the intimacy. There are even faint pencil markings on a wall, perhaps put there by a bored child. As potentially one of the most original rooms in Manhattan, it provides insight into the world these people lived in.

Perhaps even more stark is the realization none of the parishioners can see the galleries. One is in the back —invisible. Even the narrow, crooked stairs leading to the galleries are outside the main entrance so slaves would never even enter the nave of the church.

The galleries' origin and actual use is as complex as the history of slavery in America.

St. Augustine (Then The All Saints Free Church) was completed in 1828, one year after slavery was abolished in New York. So it is impossible to know just how many slaves actually used the galleries. Slaves from the South visiting New York City with their masters may have worshipped there, as well as local indentured servants. However it is a moot point for many churches in this era that built "slave galleries." They were not merely used by slaves but named as such a catch all phrase as a place to put black parishioners. Consider also when this church was planned, it was perhaps not thought slavery was going to end anytime soon.

As the years went by and the galleries' purpose slowly eroded away, the rooms were not really forgotten, just ignored. Penny King, event coordinator for the church says, "It may have been out of shame, it was a past church members wanted to forget."

But these days the church's mission is to get more visitors to the church and galleries. Minnie and Penny worry that with the current gentrification of the Lower East Side, the history could be lost. Penny says, "A lot of our parishioners who know this history are the older, black population from the neighborhood who are not being replaced by a newer generation, so we want to keep this history around."

ST. AUGUSTINE OF HIPPO EPISCOPAL CHURCH

St. Augustine of Hippo Episcopal Church is the fifth oldest church in New York City. At one time, Poet Edgar Allan Poe was said to sometimes even come inside and think in the back pews. It was said he was fond of the quietness and calmness of the church.

As for the slave galleries, they are said to have been used by at least one fugitive of the law. The story goes that New York's most notorious political party boss and just plain crook William "Boss" Tweed supposedly hid out in the slave galleries so he could attend his mother's funeral. Apparently someone tipped off the police and he narrowly escaped by climbing out of one of the church's windows. Although some dispute the tale, saying the time of his mother's death was not a time he was in need of alluding authorities. Still some surmise he may have used the slave galleries to avoid press and others who may have wanted to find him.

SNIFFEN COURT

Murray Hill is a quiet respite from Midtown Manhattan's kinetic pace. There is an air of 19th-Century charm situated within the well-maintained townhouse residences that dot the streets here. But it is a tiny private gated alleyway just off 36th Street near Third Avenue called Sniffen Court that most preserves a slice of Olde New York in Midtown Manhattan.

Sniffen Court consists of two rows of ten, mostly former carriage houses fit snuggly along a shale paved road. All of them are wonderfully maintained, almost too picturesque for their own good. The quietness of the spot is remarkable, despite being just steps from a major city avenue.

Because the gates are locked, residents are afforded a few more freedoms than their outer neighbors. For instance, normal residential fronts have an assortment of ornamentation like wreaths and well-manicured potted plants along the curbs. Outdoor knick-knacks like ornamental shoe scrapers or lawn ornaments are displayed without fear of theft. Many of the buildings have (gasp!) regular good old-fashioned window pane glass with no bars or security grating.

Cast finials shaped like horses on the front gate are a tipoff to Sniffen's past. At one time this was a mews, consisting of a row of stable carriage houses which serviced the nearby townhouses in Murray Hill. The stables were built between 1863-1864 in a Romanesque Revival style with large arched doors for the carriages, some of which are still there today. Mews were often built away from the townhouses so owners could avoid

the smell and noise common to stables. The horsemen often lived in the carriage houses upstairs in tiny apartments, always on call for their employers and horses.

Sniffen Court was named after a local builder, John Sniffen. Why it is named after him is a bit of a mystery. City records show no indication he built or owned any of the stables.

As the 20th-Century rolled in, the carriages slowly lost their purpose with the advent of the automobile and up until the 1920s some of the stables still housed horses. Now the buildings have been lovingly repurposed as homes, many closely resembling their original outer facade.

Sniffen Court has attracted quite a few notable residents over the years, like comedian "Professor" Irwin Corey, model Claudia Schiffer, and musician Lenny Kravitz. Composer Cole Porter lived in the corner townhouse at 156 E 36th Street for a time. These days the buildings go for several million dollars despite their small square footage, and they rarely change ownership.

The court seems to attract artists of different disciplines. One unique resident is the Amateur Comedy Club, a theatrical group which bought two of the stables in 1918. Sculptors Malvina Hoffman and Harriet Whitney Frishmuth also both had studios here. Two of Hoffman's works can actually still be seen through the gates in the back of the court adorning her former studio. They are of two bas-relief statues of Greek Horsemen.

A bit of rock history also took place at Sniffen Court in 1967 when the band The Doors used it as a backdrop of the cover art for their album *Strange Days*. The cover art features various circus folk characters performing their acts.

With all this history and its picturesque homes, it is no surprise Sniffen Court was put on the National Register of Historic Places in 1973. Alas, no one is allowed in Sniffen Court except residents and their guests, but perhaps that is part of its allure; a window into another time, gated off from the hustle and bustle of the city.

DOG CARRIAGE HOUSE

Just a couple of blocks down from Sniffen Court is another carriage house which has been turning heads for over a century. Carriage houses were not necessarily considered works of architectural beauty, but rather more utilitarian in nature. So the George S. Bowdoin stable on 38th Street is particularly striking.

The Dutch revival themed building, an obvious nod to the city's Dutch origins, was built in 1902 for real estate developer William Martin by architect Ralph S. Thompson.

It features a dramatic Dutch style stepped gable, but is particularly loved for its delightful stone facades of two horses and a bull dog.

In 1907 George Bowdoin bought the building and it stayed in the family until 1944. At one point it was converted into a garage before a living space and eventually an art gallery.

SPEAKEASIES

The Speakeasy moniker is thrown around a bit too often these days. Usually it is some downtown bar with a gimmick either of not having a name on the front, it is behind a hidden door in a bakery or is by invitation only. Obviously with prohibition being over and done with for decades now, by definition no true speakeasies still exists. However there are a few former ones still in business with all of their wonderful patina and authenticity gloriously intact.

WILLIAM BARNACLE TAVERN

On the outskirts of St. Marks Place is just such a spot, the William Barnacle Tavern. This former speakeasy has so much originality and lore from the prohibition era one will think alcohol is still illegal; evidence of its past is everywhere. There is the original hidden entrance, escape tunnels, and even a safe that was once loaded with millions of dollars. (We'll get to that later.) There are even remnants of booby traps in case the place was raided. (Don't worry, they have long since been deactivated.)

Called Scheib's when it was a speakeasy, it was named after Walter Scheib who was the front man for mobster, Frank Hoffman, who was the boss and real owner. Back then, patrons would go to a nearby butcher shop and ask for Scheib. From there they were led through the alleyway to a door with a hatch. Just like in movies, when the password was given, the patrons were let in.

The bar's 1920s era decor still has the vibe of an under the radar place as if a raid could still be eminent. A bit of an air of mystery and forbiddance fills the space.

It is dark, sparsely furnished and everything looks, and probably is, original. Like the original Cuban Mahogany bar, a rarity anywhere, it still has that classic Jazz age feel. Behind the bar was a small dance hall, long since gone, but after its speakeasy days it became a jazz club called the Jazz Gallery. It hosted performers like John Coltrane, Harry "Sweets" Edison and Frank Sinatra.

Much of the success of Scheib's was thanks to its direct connection to what was known as Rum Row. This was an off-shore throughway on the North Atlantic Ocean stretching from Boston to Atlantic City—25 miles out to sea in international waters, controlled by the mob for importing booze to the city. Cops on the take got 3 dollars for every 6 bottles delivered to Scheib's. They even went so far as to block off streets so the feds couldn't get near deliveries. The place was so lucrative, gangster Al Capone, made it a stop during his trips to New York City for business and pleasure. And pleasure there was, besides the stage, there was entertaining going on upstairs too. Ladies of the night were said to have quite a booming business.

With all this illicit activity going on owners took precautions some might think as overkill. In the basement there are still parts of tunnels dug to ferry in booze and for quick getaways. Entrances, passageways, and windows show evidence of steel security bars. An original wooden phone system is still in the same place to alert of any would-be raids. Perhaps expected, is a bullet hole near a money drop in the side of the wall. A bit more disturbing are the remnants of a carefully hidden thin copper wire along a window. The story goes, if a raid was imminent the copper wire connection would be broken, triggering explosives, and who knows what kind of damage. Seeing the never used thin wire is chilling—these people meant business.

The preservation of all these mobster artifacts is largely due to the place being under ownership of one family since 1964. The Otway family has preserved the place without messing with its authenticity. Howard Otway was given a mortgage by Walter Scheib who expected him to default. Scheib knew his boss Hoffman left millions in the safe in the basement and he needed a patsy and Otway, also a poor working actor, and writer fit the bill. This is where the story seems out of the pages of a gangster tale. Howard and his son, Lorcan, were cleaning out the basement when they found not one but two locked safes. Lorcan says, "My father called Mister Scheib and told him about the safes, admitting to him, 'I was too curious to leave them closed, but too cautious to open them without you.' Scheib brought in a safe cracker and while one was empty, the other

incredibly had some $1 million dollars in $100 bills. The finder's fee? The Otway's got to keep the building free and clear.

Even without it's speakeasy past, the place is loaded with history. The 1850s-era townhouse shows evidence of previous occupants like the hearth in the basement when it was a family home. In the basement are also original foundations from 17th century Dutch settlements.

Next door and now part of the William Barnacle Tavern is the 80 St. Marks Theatre, a place which has seen its share of theatrical history. This well respected off-Broadway venue has hosted numerous well-known plays and musicals like, *You're a Good Man Charlie Brown* which got its start here. Actor Billy Crystal once worked at the theatre, not as a performer, but as an usher.

Today the bar is open and available for drinks. And though alcohol is legal, customers can still walk on the wild side with their well-known selection of decadent Absinthe liquor. They have almost two dozen different brands. They are also known of course for their prohibition era cocktails.

THE BACKROOM

The Backroom can not only tout itself as a modern speakeasy, but it also as a direct descendant of those during prohibition––a lineage very few places even in New York City can attest to. It has historic DNA, for these very walls were once a prohibition-era speakeasy called, "The back of Ratner's." Ratner's was actually a well-known kosher restaurant which at the time was doing business in the front. The property was originally owned by reputed mobster, Meyer Lansky, and up until a few years ago was even still owned by his descendants.

Visiting the Backroom today is done the same way it was back then. On the Lower East Side at Norfolk Street, a small restaurant sits next door to somewhat shabby business front with the name "Lower East Side Toy Company." It is all a ruse, for there is no such business. Off to its side is a narrow steel staircase leading to what seems like the basement. However at the bottom is a long, lower-level alley that is somewhat dark and foreboding. It leads to a large courtyard surrounded by neighboring buildings. Off to the side is another metal staircase with a large black door fashioned with a peephole. Ah-ha! This is the place, but not so fast, one must have the password. (Hint: it is posted daily on their Facebook and Twitter pages.)

Say the password and you're greeted by one of the establishment's friendly bouncers.

Though most speakeasies were basically hole-in-the-walls due to their short lives and being a constant target of authorities, The Backroom has spared customers squalor surroundings. Instead, it is a feast for the eyes, a two-tiered space decorated in a gilded age meets jazz age splendor––good enough for Al Capone himself. Period furniture and fixtures highlight the look and feel along with chandeliers, velvet wallpaper, and old paintings of scantily clad ladies. The space also features the original bar, an old cigarette dispenser, and a Mutoscope showing short films. Adding to its speakeasy credo is a secret room hidden behind a swinging bookcase. Inside is an even cozier area complete with a small bar and a wonderful copper-clad ceiling.

Of course, no speakeasy would be respectable if it served its drinks in a conventional manner. Just like in prohibition days, cocktails are served in teacups and saucers while bottles of beer are handed out in paper bags. The Backroom has such authentic era feel that it has been used as a backdrop for photoshoots, movies and TV productions including *Boardwalk Empire*.

Remnants of its speakeasy past are still present including walled up secret passages and an escape hatch in the ceiling.

STATEN ISLAND
BOAT GRAVEYARD

Marine scrap yards are not a likely place ordinary folks want to spend their leisure time. But for decades people have been risking life and limb, and even spending a night in jail to take a gander at Staten Island's Arthur Kill Ship graveyard. Also known as the Witte Boneyard, it is a place that once people hear about it, they have to see it themselves despite the long trek and unwelcoming atmosphere of the place.

These half sunken hulls of rusted metal and decayed wood offer a haunting look at what was once state of the art ships.

Over forty acres of waterway, dozens of boats of all shapes and sizes have been left here to rot. Some with legendary tales, other just simply ran out their usefulness.

The vessels lay in southwestern Staten Island in the waterway of Arthur Kill. "Kill" is Dutch for "creek," though today the spot hardly conjures up creek-like imagery. A tidal strait separating Staten Island from New Jersey, Arthur Kill's shores are riddled with industrial facilities; all standard landscape in any metropolitan area except for it extraordinary boatyard.

Kayakers often paddle through the waterway for a closer gander, which is perfectly legal as long as they do not get too close. On the water, it is eerily calm and quiet. One can hear the water gently lapping against very oxidized, often jagged hulls, just skeletons now of their once purposeful days. On foot or by land, one will find an array

of ships, ferries, tugboats, barges, and even a submarine. Some are well over a hundred years old.

Will Van Dorp, who created a documentary on the ships along with Gary Kane, calls it an, "accidental marine museum." For amateur urban archeology explorers it is one New York City's must-sees. He says, "It's not so much the fact that these hulks of ships and boats are rotting and rusting; it's that they display a beauty in that state of decay that makes me wonder what beauties they manifested when they were new and functional and filled with the hopes of their crews and owners. This display excites my imagination in the same way that autumn colors do."

But it is certainly not a welcoming place. From the road there is nary a spot to take a look-see. Twelve-foot solid fencing fortresses the scrapyard yards from the shore. There are plenty of "No Trespassing" signs with various threats peppering the property. The lack of hospitality is certainly not unwarranted by the current owners, Donjon Recycling. People on a regular basis stupidly climb these decaying vessels. Their unstable hulls and decks are precariously weak and unstable through exposure and the passage of time. Jagged metal pieces peer just below the surface almost like land mines just waiting to claim a kayak or inflatable raft. Incredibly, one woman waded through the water naked to have photos of herself on the wrecks as part of an art project. For pedestrians, the Rossville cemetery just down the road gives a bit of a view but nothing compared to being on the water itself. But the intriguing headstones are interesting alone.

The boatyard was never meant to become so big. It started when John J. Witte began buying up obsolete boats in the 1930s. He became a nautical hoarder, accumulating vessels but not dismantling them for scrap. Instead he waited for potential buyers for salvage parts. Then came the end of World War II and a deluge of vessels retiring from military service was added to the collection. Witte died in 1980 leaving what has been called the legacy of the world's largest depository of historic ships.

Now with it under Donjon Recycling some 400 ships have dwindled down to less than a hundred.

But the yard still draws crowds who are fascinated by these rusting, twisted, dejected looking vessels. Charter boats even make it part one of their stops as part of their sightseeing itinerary. Something that would probably irritate the living daylights out of John Witte. (He was known to aggressively chase people out of the area himself.)

Among the more notable ships is USS PC-1264; a World War II submarine chaser, which was the first to have a mostly

African-American crew. There is the Abram S. Hewitt fireboat, which served as command post during the sinking of the PS General Slocum which claimed over a thousand lives—the city's most deadly disaster before September 11, 2001.

One vessel, *YOG-64*, was even exposed to radioactive fallout. This Navy gas tanker was posted in 1948 during the Operation Sandstone nuclear tests in the Bikini Atoll.

As the remaining ships quietly rot away and are being slowly disassembled, their disintegration and disappearance may be the only thing that will finally stop the curious from visiting this out of the way place in Staten Island.

BLAZING STAR CEMETERY

Several yards from one of the only places one can see bits of the boat graveyard, from the shore, sits is a small ancient cemetery. Mere inches from the edge of Arthur Kill Road, the Blazing Star Cemetery looks completely out of place among the auto repair shops and industrial facilities. It is a poignant example of life and progress doing what it always does—moving on.

This neighborhood was known in the mid-18th century as Old Blazing Star after a local tavern. It was also a popular ferry crossing with some vessels going even as far as Philadelphia.

Today the cemetery is barely noticeable from the road. Its graves is obscured in a partially wooded area with headstones going back at least to 1751. Some have wonderful iconography typical of colonial times.

Blazing Star Cemetery is thought to be an old family burial ground for the Slaight Dutch family. Later other families were buried there like the Marshalls, Poillon and Ayers, Deckers—familiar names in Staten Island history. The last burial took place in 1865.

TWA FLIGHT CENTER

Once upon a time air travel was a rarified and dignified experience, unlike today which can feel akin to riding on a bus. The "Jet Age" in the early 1960s was a time when the actual travel was almost as exciting as the destination. Nowhere to be found were the everlasting lines at the TSA, food courts with flat food, or fellow passengers in flip flops and t-shirts.

At the JFK International Airport in Queens, New York, there are remnants of those high flying days. Locked up and mothballed for years, The TWA Flight Center has not seen any passengers for years, yet it still captures the imagination and whimsical fancy when catching a glimpse of it while riding between terminals. A touchstone of the Mid-century Modern design movement, it may be getting a second act soon enough.

The TWA Flight Center, also known as the Trans World Flight Center, was designed by Eero Saarinen. The Finnish-American architect, who's name even has a futuristic ring to it, was known for his neo-futuristic designs which include the St. Louis arch in Missouri and the Dulles International Airport in Washington DC. Saarinen even designed the beloved Knoll brand "Tulip" chair.

His inspiration for the TWA Flight center was the shape of a bird in flight. The actual building he created is under the shape of the curved wings and swooping body. Large open spaces giveing the structure a light, airy look and feel. Structural lines throughout the building continually lift one's eyes upwards contributing to the graceful theme.

Everything has the look of movement—from the windows pushing outward, to the curved staircases and balconies, one would be hard pressed to find a ninety degree angle. The centerpiece is the sunken lounge waiting area in the middle of the building. It is punctuated with bright red seats which offered front row seats to the comings and goings on the airport's runways.

But Saarinen's vision wasn't limited to just *looking* futuristic, he also incorporated elements and designs he thought would make the building more efficient and less cumbersome. He did this by using a "plate and shell" design for the main structure. This enabled wide and open spaces while still using lightweight materials. A thin layer of concrete reinforced with rebar allows the shell sections of the roof to stand freely without the need of columns to holding it up. Similar to an airplane fuselage or boat hull, this gives the structure its unique strength and wide open space.

The flight center was also one of the first commercial terminals to be in an all enclosed space. Also, the terminal gates being placed in a satellite formation away from the main terminal, give a more orderly approach to aircraft management. This type of formation paved the way for other terminals to adopt it in the oncoming years.

The innovations did not end there, an electronic departure and arrival board, baggage carousels, and closed circuit TV were also firsts for this "Jet Age" pioneer.

Sadly, Saarien died suddenly in 1961, one year before The TWA Flight Center opened. He was awarded posthumously the AIA Gold Medal for the design of his inventive terminal.

Ironically, the Flight Center quickly had trouble keeping up with the fast growing jet age it helped usher in. Newer jumbo jets were too big for the terminal, plus heightened airport security and increased passenger traffic all contributed to its demise.

TWA eventually went out of business and American Airlines took over the space, closing the terminal for good in 2001.

It would be very easy to demolish such a utilitarian and valuable piece of property at JFK airport. But through the years the public has always had an affinity for the Flight Center. Designated a NYC landmark in 1994 and put on the National Register of Historic Places in 2005, the Port Authority of New York and New Jersey who governs the space looked for years for a creative way to reinvigorate it. Parts of the building were first preserved when JetBlue Airlines built a new terminal in the area and incorporated some of the old Flight Center into their terminal.

Now it looks like the main structure will open again. MCR Development has stepped in with bold plans to convert the building and the surrounding area into a 505 room hotel which will incorporate a conference area and observation deck. (Oddly enough, JFK has no hotels on its premises.) The main center will be preserved as close to its heyday as possible. Though airports are usually for coming and going, MCR is determined in making this a place people will want to come and visit. The entire facility will be made to handle special events and will be easily accessible to the public.

POPE'S CHAIR

With being a world class terminal, it comes as no surprise the TWA Flight Center saw its share of celebrities and dignitaries. One in particular caused great excitement. There is even a memento of the visit still at the Flight Center.

October 4, 1965, Pope Paul IV flew directly from Rome, Italy to JFK Airport. The trip was beyond historic for not only was it the first time a Pope had left Italy since 1809, he was the first Pope ever to visit the Western Hemisphere. Though Pope Paul IV was only on the ground for fourteen hours, he managed to be seen by an estimated one million people that day while only visiting New York City.

After a series of events and meetings which included addressing the United Nations and talking with President Lyndon B. Johnson, the Pontiff conducted Mass for thousands at Yankee Stadium.

When it was time to return to Rome, TWA had the honor of taking him back. They outfitted a special plane with a bed, conference room and perhaps the best amenity—more legroom between the seats. When the Pope arrived at the Flight Center, waiting for him in one of the upper lounge was a special seat outfitted with a small table in the center. It is said this is where his holiness met with his final guests and waited for his departure to take him back to Rome. Even today the seat is referred to as the "Pope's Chair."

WASHINGTON SQUARE VAULTS

Washington Square Park is the very definition of Greenwich Village. For generations of New Yorkers it has been a place of cultural liveliness and vitality, while also a welcoming repose from the city's sometimes cold and detached surroundings. But few today who enjoy the park's confines have any idea of what is just mere feet below them. Human remains from perhaps tens of thousands of souls.

Since the 17th Century, parts of park and the surrounding areas have been used for a variety of things, including farming, a homestead for freed slaves, military parade grounds. It was even a burial ground, which even today will sometimes reveal itself.

On November 5, 2015 workers for the New York City Department of Design and Construction were replacing a century old water main pipeline at Wooster Street on Washington Square East. Upon digging, they struck a brick arch formation just three and a half feet from street level. It ended up being the top of one of two vaults; both around fifteen by twenty feet in size and eight feet deep and constructed of brick and whitewashed fieldstone walls.

Archeologists from Chrysalis Archaeological Consultants were brought in to access the structures and try to gleam any historic information from them. Part of their results revealed the two vaults contained remains of church members from two former neighborhood congregations—Cedar Street and Pearl Street churches.

Oddly after the discovery of the vault, just a little research yielded a New York Times article from 1965 which reported one of these same vaults being uncovered during a dig done by ConEdison.

They also manage to carefully take a small stone out of one of the walls and use a camera with a telephoto lens to take pictures inside the vault. The results were grim but not unexpected. Some coffins were severely deteriorated and skeletal remains were strewn all over. However, around twenty coffins were in surprisingly good shape. Some were adorn with small metal nameplates with the names of the deceased. Smaller coffins in the vault tell a grim truth of early nineteenth century life; loss of a child from illness or disease was commonplace.

As for the vaults and the remains, they will stay just as they are, untouched which is city policy and just simply respectful.

The discovery was unexpected but not surprising. At one time some two-thirds of Washington Square Park and the area surrounding was a potter's field. Some 20,000 people are estimated to have been interred there for about 30 years right after the Revolutionary War. Often the deceased were victims of yellow fever.

Even today every so often human bone fragments will turn up in the park during routine maintenance and restoration.

WOOLWORTH BUILDING

One of the casualties of September 11th, 2001 was the closing of some of the city's great spaces. Because of security concerns many buildings and lobbies are now off limits to the masses for which they were ultimately designed for in the first place. Some of the best architecture and design in the world are now hidden from the most appreciative eyes.

Perhaps the saddest of all is the Woolworth Building on 233 Broadway in the heart of Downtown Manhattan, mere steps from the World Trade Center. Inside and out, The Woolworth is a gilded age temple still turning heads at over a hundred years old.

Five and dime store magnate, F. W. Woolworth, wanted his world headquarters to look similar to French cathedrals and the houses of Parliament in London, England. Designed in a neo-gothic style by famed architect, Cass Gilbert, Woolworth chose the proper architect. Gilbert was well-respected for his pioneering designs and willingness to take bold chances. Cass would also design the U.S. Supreme Court Building, Minnesota State Capitol, and United States Customs House among others.

Woolworth, ever the taskmaster, was intently involved with the design and construction, even deciding on items like hallway and bathroom fixtures. This extra attention seemed to have helped since the building is dripping with ornamental details. The exterior, which is a combination of white limestone and clad terra cotta panels, ascend unobstructed almost to the top, giving the building a soaring design much like